Edward Garnett

The Paradox Club

Edward Garnett

The Paradox Club

ISBN/EAN: 9783743308695

Manufactured in Europe, USA, Canada, Australia, Japa

Cover: Foto ©Thomas Meinert / pixelio.de

Manufactured and distributed by brebook publishing software
(www.brebook.com)

Edward Garnett

The Paradox Club

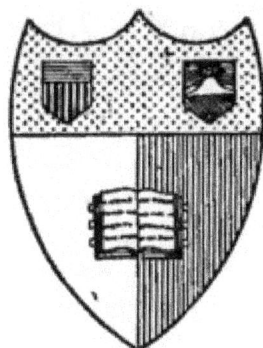

THE PARADOX CLUB

THE
PARADOX CLUB

BY

EDWARD GARNETT

"ἀτοπωτάτους δή τινας ἴσως δοκῶ σοι
λέγειν. ἔντυχοι μεντᾶν τις ἐν τῇ πόλει
τοῖς τοιούτοις. οἵοις ἐμοί τε καὶ σοί."
—Ἀπολλοδώρου του κουφολογου περι
ματαιοτεχνιας· κεφ.δ.

London
T. FISHER UNWIN
26 PATERNOSTER SQUARE
MDCCCLXXXVIII

To ——

Of what may not be broken,
And what must not be spoken,
Be this to thee the token.

CONTENTS.

———◆———

"*THE WINDSOR CASTLE.*"

2

THE PARADOX CLUB.

I.

"*THE WINDSOR CASTLE.*"

THE flash of a carriage-lamp in a dark street lit up for an instant two faces, and revealed two people to one another.

"Patrick!"

"Nina!"

"Who would ever have thought of meeting you here?"

The young man and young woman, who had thus met by accident in the Hammersmith Broadway, turned in towards the Windsor Castle.

It was a warm Sunday night in June,

and the roadway was studded with little groups of people who stood gossiping in shadow. A fruit-shop hard by cast a solitary bright patch across the pavement, and here the passers-by stepped into existence for a few yards of light, and then stepped quietly out of it again. Strings of men and women arm in arm, soldiers—spots of scarlet—sailors with bronzed faces, smiling girls in pink, moved in front of the flaring gas like a stream of marionettes and then vanished to be seen no more.

On the night wind came floating the sound of a horn far away. Tra la la, tria tira tria la. Nearer and nearer it came, and with it the quick beat of hoofs and the thunder of wheels. Close at hand it seemed to be; now round the bend of the road it swept; and now the people had barely time - to gain the causeway when an omnibus, drawn by three horses, dashed past the Windsor

Castle. Opposite the bracket of lights where swung the sign-board, the people on the top of the coach could be seen laughing and chatting ; the next instant they were swallowed up in the darkness, and the horn was already sounding far away down the street. The talkers moved back into the roadway and took up their conversation where they had left off.

The Windsor Castle stands a little way back from the other houses, and has an air of respectability and solidity peculiar to an inn that scrutinizes its visitors before they can come to close quarters. Nina and Patrick brushed past an old ostler who stood before a pyramid of green buckets, watching with melancholy eyes for an ideal four-in-hand that never came ; and began to pace up and down the yard, over the cobbles, in the shadow of the inn. A Salvationist had taken possession of the darkest corner, but he was reserving his eloquence for the benefit of a celebrated local Atheist who was momentarily expected.

"Then you have been abroad all this time?" asked Patrick.

"O no! I have been in London for the last four months. And you?"

"I expect to die a clerk," he answered; "for I am still working at the office. But what an odd meeting-place! How did you come here?"

"Oh," said Nina, "we have always been meeting in odd places ever since we were children. How curious it was, for instance, that your family and mine should have written for the same house at such an out-of-the-way place as Morthoe?"

"My mother always declares there is an affinity between the Lindons and the Welds," said Patrick. "And at any rate both homes broke up about the same time."

"Come, let us leave old times alone," cried Nina. "Why is it that when people get together again, they always go over the same old ground? I hate the past, especially since my father's death. Let us talk about the present; so tell me where you are living now? Are you still on your beloved Surrey side?"

"I have taken a garret in Ivy Lane."

"Ivy Lane! Why that is where the Paradox Club meets! You know I am a member."

"I had heard about the Club in a vague way from somebody or other; but I had no idea that it was so near me. How is it that you belong to it? I thought a Club that tried so hard to be original must be necessarily dull."

"It amuses me," she answered; "and it has many advantages. To belong to it is the easiest possible way of breaking with all one's relations. A social Club that has rooms in one end of the town instead of the other, that meets at ten instead of the fashionable eight, that includes women as well as men, is so absolutely incomprehensible to the average mind that all its members are obviously outside Society. To the few friends who really care for me it doesn't matter a pin if I do what I like; but to most of my acquaintances it makes all the difference in the world whether a woman goes where she pleases."

" But still," urged Patrick, "it is unpleasant for all one's friends to talk about one, and say how sad it is that Nina should—etc."

" No. They leave off talking, and drop you altogether," said Nina ; "and so you get rid of the people who, on the strength of having been introduced to you, think they have a right to criticize in detail everything you do. Besides there are many advantages. I never used to go about London before,"

"But surely you needn't join the Paradox Club in order to go about London alone?"

"Oh, I don't go alone!"

"Does the Club then ramble about in a body?"

"We sometimes branch off into twos and threes. I have been seeing something of Mr. Martell lately."

Patrick shrugged his shoulders.

"I think I should like to belong," he said, "just for the fun of the thing."

"What a capital idea! And we want a new member. Everybody else is so much in earnest about things they know nothing about, that you who know a little of everything, will be a delightful change. There is a Committee Meeting to-morrow, and I will write to-night and propose you."

"But perhaps they won't have me."

"Oh, I am sure they will, because they can't find anybody to read a paper

2*

for next week, and one was promised. Now, if you will make one up, they will be delighted to let you in, especially as they know I shouldn't introduce anybody very stupid. You will like it, I know, because we talk of everything under the sun, and have at last nearly got to the point when nobody is offended at anything that is said."

"But what on earth shall I write about?" he asked.

"Take that for your moral," said Nina, pointing to a 'bus-driver who was gallantly kissing his hand towards an upper window in the inn, where fluttered a white dress. They watched till the girl re-appeared in the doorway, and ran to join her lover under a dark archway.

"How happy she is!" said Nina, with the faintest touch of sadness in her voice.

"Do you remember that evening at Porlock?" began Patrick, eagerly, looking up only to meet with a laugh from Nina.

" I always feel a little sentimental on Sunday night, don't you ? " she said. " I put it down to the approach of Black Monday, and the week's work."

Patrick was too angry to speak. He vowed, for not the first time, that he would never allude to Porlock again.

" What a fool I am," he thought, " to keep on pretending to myself she cares for me. I will never be sentimental with her again, never ! "

" I will write a paper on Women and Men," he said presently, changing his tone so successfully that Nina knew it was put on, " and I will praise the men so much that all the women will get indignant, and there will be a battle-royal."

" Yes, praise the men ; for that will irritate Mr. Chapple dreadfully. Mr. Chapple is a misandrist," she explained,

" who will amuse you as much at first as he will bore you afterwards."

"And your misogynist?"

"Is Mr. Martell, a Socialist whose theories will not irritate you so much as his pessimism."

"Does he amuse you?"

"No," said Nina, laughing, "I amuse him."

"What business has the fellow to be amused with her!" thought Patrick; but he said aloud, "Who are the other celebrities of the Club?"

"There is Mr. McWhirter, a Scotchman, of whom I can only that if it was a paradox to admit him, it would certainly be a platitude to turn him out. Then there is the poet, Lofthouse, who, his enemies say, is a living argument that Swinburne should never have come into existence."

"How so?' asked Patrick.

"Well, they say that if he had not

Swinburne's metres to copy he would imitate Browning, and so be unintelligible.   He is warm-hearted, though, and I expect you will like him.   Then there is my friend, Charlotte Ward, of whom I will say nothing, Mrs. Lucas, Edward Brinton, and several others.   There are two members who never by any chance speak, and two others to whom nobody listens."

"A pretty mixed lot!   And you meet in Ivy Lane?"

"Yes," she replied, "poor little place, it is fast growing respectable!   Still it is near the river which you were so fond of and I found so dull."

"You are just as bad as all the rest," he declared.   "I never knew a woman yet who cared for the picturesque."

"You always said that to annoy me, whereas I expect I know more picturesque scenes than you.   Now have you ever stood on London Bridge and watched the sun rise?"

" No, I haven't ; have you ?"

"Well, not yet," she admitted, "but I mean to."

" People say," added Patrick, "that you can't have anything duller than the London streets, but thanks to our Vestries, you have roads up everywhere ; and by night there are the red lamps, the wigwams and the charcoal fires of the workmen.   From Chiswick to the docks the Thames presents hundreds of studies in cloud, sky, and water, ever shifting in sunshine and rain.   The weather that we are always cursing creates a thousand effects of light and shade on the river, and a fog in Cheapside means rolling and lifting masses of mist at London Bridge."

"Ah," said Nina, with a little yawn, " I knew you would get on capitally with Lofthouse.   He is always lecturing us on our blindness."   Then womanlike, a little sorry at having shown she was bored, she hastened to add, "I think we have found the picturesque here."

Patrick looking back saw the yard was full of strange shadows. From a cart where flared a fierce white light a bare-headed man was thundering away to a highly appreciative audience below. On the skirt of the crowd stood a little wizened old woman intently watching the Atheist's face, which was red with laughter and excitement. Not a movement escaped this Christian cat, sure of her atheistical mouse. Her fixed eyes and withered face said clearly what her thin lips only muttered—

"You think yourself very clever with your low jokes at the Holy Bible ; but you will burn in Hell for this, my fine fellow, for ever and ever, some day."

Presently the Salvationists in the darkest corner of the yard broke into a quiet hymn, which rising sad and low made the world fade for a little while to those who stood and listened. But the beer-drinkers lounging on the tavern steps paid not the slightest attention. They did not even seem to be aware of the presence of either Atheist or Salvationist, and gazed at the starry night with the air of sceptics who doubted the reality of all things save horse-flesh. Nothing affected them but the absence of liquor; and they measured time by the number of quarts. As children turn the hour-glass upside down when the sand has all run through, and let a little run back again, they held their glasses downwards, and waiting till the froth had trickled on to the ground, they sighed quietly and turned back into the bar for another pint of "four-half." Every Sunday night in summer they came to smoke, drink, and bet in a quiet way, and they always encountered the preacher. Too much of even salvation palls. The hymn rose louder and louder and seemed to speak so confidently of a life hereafter that many of the Atheist's hearers became uneasy, and, thinking it better to be on the safe side, turned towards the Salvationists. Others suddenly remembering that infidelity is hardly respectable on Sunday evening, stole silently away. But the Atheist held his ground with the confidence of a man who knows how to pick conundrums from the Bible, and demonstrated triumphantly to a few faithful followers that it was superfluous for Noah to place a pair of fleas in the Ark.

Nina and Patrick left the rivals for popularity, and turned to examine the inn that encourages all sects because "preaching is thirsty work." A glance round the bar, of an afternoon, reveals the mother-o'-pearl buttons, the ashplants, and the bow-legs of a generation that one fancied had long ago passed away. The farmers, however, after the

Saturday night's dissipation, had all returned home that morning with their empty hay-carts, and Nina and Patrick found an almost empty bar. Two women were leaning against the counter, and admiring a little curly haired boy whose head was buried in a quart-pot which his mother held for him to drink from. Presently he dived under the arms of the three gaitered stable-boys leaning stick in hand against the door-way, and darted across the dark yard to join some barefooted little girls, dressed in straight faded purple gowns, who stood in a silent row before the fruiterers shop, and eyed the piles of bigaroon cherries that smiled crimson and white in the gaslight. When a passer-by bought some the children stretched out their hands, but said not a word ; and when a cherry or two was dropped into their tiny palms, they eat them slowly and solemnly to make them last as long as possible. Soon they could bear to look at the tantalizing fruit no longer, and they slipped back to the yard with its lights and shadows to play a silent hide and seek, stealing in and out of the crowd like little mice, and running round the pyramid of green buckets where the old ostler stood watching them with a melancholy smile. Round and round, and in and out of the shadows they ran, indifferent to all that was going on, to the fanaticism of the preacher, to the logic of the Atheist, to the rolling choruses that resounded down the Broadway from the throats of the pleasure-seekers, happy and careless after the long summer day.

"I understand, to-night, the philosophers who say that the world is not real at all," said Patrick.

"What a shock the man who first discovered that must have felt!" laughed Nina.

" Nothing seems real to me here. So many opposites collected in this yard seem to destroy one another. The Atheist who looks on the Salvationist as a fool is thought to be the Devil by that old woman there. Nobody notices the children who will be singing hymns or roaring songs on this very spot when the present generation is dead, which will be in less than thirty years! What a pretty girl that was on the box-seat of the last coach that flashed by! I thought she waved her hand to me. How odd it is to think that while all these cries are rising to-night into the air the world is going round and round!"

"Come!" cried Nina, "you are getting too deep for me! When you talk of the world going round and round I feel my head swim. Do you expect the globe to stand still because those people yonder were converted so quickly? The only thing that troubles me is that we didn't give those baby-buntings some cherries."

"When you catch an Irishman moralizing," said Patrick, apologetically, "be sure he is either ripe for the grave or for bed. Let us——"

He broke off his sentence and listened to the sound that came from the Richmond Road, the sound of many voices in chorus, and the beat of many feet. As the roar died away, a single voice took up the song, rising clearly above the dull tramp, tramp, tramp. The verse lasted till the voice seemed only a few yards off in the gloom, and then the chorus burst forth again, shaking the windows, and making every stone in the Windsor Castle echo and ring. The people in the yard joined in :—

"We are four jolly good fellows, we are !
  The best of all jolly good fellows, hurrah !
  We were when we started this morning, ha, ha !
  But the rest they have all got run in ! "

closing in round the singers ; and the crowd swept by, a sea of faces under the bracket of lights, towards Kensington.

"Let us follow them," said Nina. "There is nobody left but those men who are still drinking and star-gazing, and their wives who are wondering what they can find to pawn to-morrow."

"That is my road," she said when they had reached the bottom of the Broadway. "I will not take you any further."

"If the Paradox Club accept me," said Patrick, detaining her hand for an instant, "and we see a little of London together, in what character shall we meet?"

"As friends," she answered. "Good-night."

IN DEFENCE OF WOMAN.

II.

IN DEFENCE OF WOMEN.

"Woman," said Patrick to the assembled Paradox Club, "is a diamond, adorning the wearer. View it in this light and you are dazzled by its brilliancy; in this and you are struck dumb by its whiteness and purity; in this and it blushes rose-pink, the colour of modesty. Yet there are critics who see nought in the stone but the green or yellow that is reflected from their own eyes. Some lament its sharpness, saying it cuts worse than a knife, especially when set in a ring; others deplore its hardness; but what good is it to argue with those who

3

would thus have a woman blunt, and with those who deplore her durability ?

"Woman's superiority over man has, however, been put so much in jeopardy by the rise of a class whose very existence is a satire on their sex that it is time for some one to declare the truth boldly.

"It is at best a perplexing task to select examples of man's inferiority to woman, for instances rush on one by the thousand.   Let us, merely to gain breathing-space, cry 'Beauty !'

"The sneer which most men assume to hide their mortification when they look in the looking-glass is as unavailing as the train of subterfuges that speedily follows.   It is useless for men to protest that beauty is skin-deep and that they would not have it as a gift.   Such assertions are as ridiculous as the writhings that accompany them.   The reason of man's ugliness is of course obvious.   While he has chosen wives for their beauty, he has with supreme indifference for the welfare of his descendants, not waited to be selected. Behold the results of his brutality!

" The number of ugly men that are to be met with in the streets is indeed appalling to a pretty woman. To avoid the hideous sight Beauty is often compelled to turn her head away, and thereby incur a charge of coquetry, a charge the inherent absurdity of which speaks for itself.

" That utilitarian nation, the Chinese, has a proverb to the effect that if Sing-Sing be dead it is no use to cut his head off. So leaving the horrible but undeniable fact that men are ugly, let us direct attention to their heaviness. Here a gentle hint may be given to our friends that this assertion is not to be disproved by their getting up and stamping about the room. Rather let them approach this painful subject with their boots off;

for they cannot hope to imitate successfully a woman's light footstep.

"One might as well swathe Nelson's
Column in brown paper, and then contend
it was not there, as explain away mas-
culine clumsiness by saying woman is
exceptionally deft. *Qui s'excuse s'accuse !*
In habits, language, clothing, dinners, in
fact, in everything men are heavy.
' Well, and if they are ?' cry many manly
voices ; ' Let us grant they are heavy,
what then ?' Gentlemen, having admitted the fact it is useless for you to
shut your eyes to what follows. You
are like sheep going to the slaughter
which baa contemptuously as they flock
along the road.

"Is it nothing that when some men
laugh they shake the house ? Apart
from the injury done to the foundations,
I would respectfully point out that in
man's heaviness lies the root of the
absurd accusation that women have no

sense of humour. What woman of sensibility can bear to have her wit at first misunderstood, then pounded with force into a stupid head, and finally guffawed over ? Even were there no risk of apoplexy, coarse laughter is so unspeakably revolting to the feminine mind that nothing would induce most women to venture on a joke when men are by. Unwilling, therefore, to waste their keen but delicate arrows on the tough hide of man, they reserve them for their own sex, whence springs the ancient calumny that women hate one another.

"One of the most absurd arguments ever used in support of the fiction of man's superiority is that he has held woman in subjection ever since the world began. In fancied or in real subjection?

"Woman, ages ago, finding man at her elbow, reflected, 'Behold a strong, coarse, and low creature, who has an

absurd attachment to me! It is most
fitting that he should go out in the wet
and cold, and kill savage animals for *me*
to eat, and dig the ground for *my* corn,
and cut down the forests, so that *I* may
walk easily. I will stay at home and
talk.'

"Accordingly, she at once turned man
out of doors as a sort of machine, to do
all the rough work for which her delicate
organization was not fitted. And man,
forsooth, because he was too dull to see
that he was directed by an intelligence
superior to his own, has the arrogance to
claim the mastery, in virtue of the labour
he performs!

"Now that marshes have been drained,
and ground cleared, and roads and railways made, and the world, in short,
rendered traversable, women are coming
to the front, and calmly and with dignity
dispossessing men. Their cry is no
longer, 'We are equal,' but 'We are

superior.' Though Girton has not been founded many years, it has more than once beaten Oxford and Cambridge ; though obstacles beyond number have been thrown in the way of women qualifying as doctors, the unequal conditions under which they rival male physicians show their greater capabilities.

"We have no wish to disparage men —far from it—for we believe that in secret they suffer severely from the gloom into which their obvious inferiority plunges them ; but, at the same time, it is a truer kindness to point out to them their melancholy position, than to flatter them with the delusive hope that the day is near when they may at length expect to rival woman.

"Considering the progress that the sexes have made of late, we may well exclaim with the poet :

" 'And panting man toiled after her in vain.'

Let not man, however, despair,

"Though inferior in beauty and wit, goodness and greatness (for we no more count brutality greatness than we count practical joking wit), if he unreservedly commit himself to feminine hands, he may, in time, raise himself almost to the level of one whom he has, at least, the grace to acknowledge as his better-half. Count Rumford reclaimed the beggars of Bavaria at a single stroke, and if it were not for the denseness, the stupidity of the male mind, wives might do the same with their husbands to-morrow.

"Of course we do not wish to argue for a single moment that woman has not her faults. She, alas! has many ; among which indulgence to men stands the foremost. Her heart is so large that she cannot generally bear to outshine the other sex either in business or conversation ; but let her once be aroused, and she will have her way, come what will. Indeed, a proverb to that effect exists among every nation on the face of the earth.

"Uncouth characters on the skulls of mammoths, testifying to woman's power, were deciphered by the late Frank Buckland; and was it not Mr. Thomson, the African explorer, who asserted that above the door of every Masai's hut are written the words, 'She ruleth here?' Mr. Monteiro, we believe, found the same thing in Angola; but it were an idle task to multiply instances.

"Doubtless there are some Positivists present who will speak with no uncertain sound on the illustrious Comte, and his woman-worship.

"Men say that they, and they alone have ruled the world. If this be so, can they look with pride on the results? The evils that exist now are largely caused by the hypocrisy of man, who refuses to acknowledge that he is guided by woman. This argument may be made more plain by the illustration of a vicious horse and its rider; man is the former, woman the latter, and when there is a spill we should like to know who is to blame.

"We will not, however, pursue our argument further, nor strike a man when he is down; and it is so patent that he is down that our heart is filled with pity for him. We readily grant that man is superior in battle; but what a superiority in the nineteenth century! He is also superior in politics; but woman has never fairly entered the lists with him. Some claim he may have to width of understanding; but, in trying to grasp all, he misses all. Commerce remains in the hands of man, so does the sweating system.

"But even in the stronghold of trade woman is a better bargainer than man; for, starvation apart, she will give her body and soul for a little love, but he often barters his for a little pleasure."

A murmur of applause ran round the room as Patrick concluded. The Club was in a talking humour, and most of the members coughed in the dangerous manner that indicates a person has something to say.

"All who have heard Mr. Weld's paper this evening," said a small gentleman with a pugnacious eye, "will, I am sure, join with me in assuring him of the great benefit the members individually and collectively have received. But I confess there was an absence of statistics on this most important subject, a disposition to smooth over the difficulties, I might even go further, and say a one-sidedness in a few of his statements that has disappointed me."

Patrick glanced to where Nina sat, hoping she would combat this just criticism. But she remained silent, and gazed earnestly at Chapple, as though she were drinking in all he said.

"I am of course aware," continued Chapple, with a wave of his hand, "that Mr. Weld has approached the question lightly. But it is, with all deference to him, a very bad sign for a nation not to treat Woman seriously. I have only to call your attention to the instances of Rome under the Cæsars, France under Napoleon III. ; and to contrast with such frivolous and corrupted societies that of the ancient Germans, the modern Dutch, and the Bavarians—the women of which last state it is impossible to treat frivolously—to see how important it is that the wives, the mothers, and the daughters of England should not be approached lightly."

"But *are* they approached lightly, Mr. Chapple ? " asked a young lady, in a timid voice.

"That Woman is approached lightly ? " replied the oracle, with genuine indignation, "is, I think, apparent to any

thinker who may have casually strayed
into a music hall and heard the thought-
less, not to say flippant manner, in which
she is addressed. That a youth who is
about to embark on the perilous voyage
of matrimony should address his future
companion with the appellation of ' Tart,'
varied perhaps by.——"

Nina beckoned Patrick aside to introduce him to a young man with curly
hair, who had just entered the room.
Lofthouse looked in Patrick's frank eyes
and took a fancy to him at once. He
always boasted that he followed instinct,
and a very short acquaintance with him
showed that he was not, at all events,
like Martell the Socialist, a slave of
Reason. Patrick, on his part, seeing that
Lofthouse was not a scrap in love with
Nina, felt immediately an extraordinary
sense of relief and gratitude, and was
ready to hail the young man as a friend
in the strange circle into which chance
had flung him.

"You can watch the people from here," said Lofthouse, stepping on to the little balcony outside the window, across which a curtain was half-draped; "and I will tell you a little about them."

"Who *is* that extraordinary Chapple?" asked Patrick.

" My dear fellow, I don't like to be ill-natured," replied the Poet; "but he is an unmitigated bore. His one theme is the superiority of Woman, and indeed it is whispered that he is right in attributing common-sense to her, since four have rejected him."

"And that young lady talking to him," said Patrick.

"Would like to be the fifth!" Lofthouse continued. " Miss Ward is not bad-looking to my taste, but a distinguished critic once cruelly said of her that she possessed the beauties of the mind. You must think me very ill-natured to repeat all this ? "

" Oh, not at all," said Patrick, thinking him most ill-natured.

" The fact is," pursued the Poet, " that I have a grudge against Miss Ward at the moment. The other night I was talking about Swinburne, and— well perhaps I seemed a little conceited —she made me promise I would perform any penance she might think fit to impose. What do you think it was ? "

" To repeat some of your own poetry," suggested Patrick.

" Exactly ! " replied the Poet, inno- cently. " How strange you should have hit it ! Was it not too bad of her ? "

" The worst injury you can do a poet is to read his poetry," replied Patrick, sententiously.

Lofthouse frowned.

" Never mind," said Patrick, eager to set matters straight again. " It was very malicious of her."

Lofthouse winced.

"At all events," cried the Irishman, hastily, "I shall hear some to-night, and that will show me a little of what you really think, won't it ?"

"Yes," replied the Poet, slightly in doubt as to the compliment ; "but you should have been here at the last meeting. The first poem was the best."

" Who is that man standing by himself in that corner—the man with rather a melancholy face, I mean," asked Patrick, anxious to escape from such delicate ground.

" Oh, that is Brinton. He is a very curious fellow, and I don't quite understand him. He has a history, I think ; at least I was told so. His father was of good family, but he got into difficulty, and Brinton, I believe, was brought up in quite low surroundings. He rarely alludes to it, though from what he says

you will see that he knows a great deal
of London and London life. There !
You see that dark handsome man who
is just speaking to him ? "

" The man with the black hair ? "
returned Patrick, who was on the look-
out for a rival.

" Yes. Well, he is Martell, the
Socialist. It will interest you to know
him, for Miss Lindon introduced him to
the Club, just as she has you."

" Oh, indeed ! " said Patrick, in a
voice that might have been a little
happier.

" Between you and me," whispered
Lofthouse, maliciously, who saw how the
land lay, and knew that a lover will
swallow anything, " he is a good deal in
love with her."

This was a clever invention of the
Poet's, and Patrick immediately reversed
it, and in a few minutes believed that
what the Poet had meant to say was that

Nina was a good deal in love with Martell.

"What of that gentleman with the red beard?" he said, to say something.

"That is McWhirter. I can't tell you anything about *him*. You will know soon enough," groaned Lofthouse.

"What is he?"

"Say what isn't he. Reptile! Philistine! But the extraordinary thing about him is that he is always admitted everywhere; he is always at the studios; he has always the best place at the theatre, and nobody knows why. For instance, I met him last night at Dearsley's!"

"Perhaps he went for the society one meets there."

"He went to drink the whiskey and water," said the Poet, warmly. "One merit the man has, and I believe it has ensured his introduction everywhere: he is a good listener!"

" Then you don't speak to one another,
I suppose," said Patrick.

" I don't say we are not on speaking
terms," said Lofthouse, " but I wouldn't
answer for the quality of our language.
Come, let us join the others!"

"If a man really loves a woman,"
they heard Chapple remarking, "the
best way he can show it is by not
marrying her."

" Most women would think that
pushing kindness a little too far," said
Nina; " though of course they would be
very grateful for such consideration."

" But do not you think, Miss Lindon,
that as we have reached a stage when
every cultured man feels himself utterly
unworthy of the woman he loves, the
time is approaching when he will have
the courage to sacrifice himself to his
convictions, and refuse to drive a woman
to the degradation of marrying her
inferior ? "

"But," urged Nina, gravely, "many noble women — indeed most of my intimate friends—are eager to make the experiment, and see whether they cannot raise men, and give them loftier ideals."

"Ah, most gratifying!" murmured Chapple.

"And several who have tried," she continued, "assure me that they do not regret the step, for though they have, as you say, in a manner thrown themselves away, still they have made their husbands happy, in which they find their own happiness."

"Still, to a woman who contemplates a career, marriage means a sad, an utter waste of time."

"My married friends say," pursued Nina, "that there is not so much time wasted as one might think."

"You talk of a career!" broke in Lofthouse, contemptuously. "What on earth does a woman want with a career at all? Not one in a thousand prefers a profession to marriage."

"You forget you are in the nineteenth century," said Chapple, severely. "Remember that there *are* women who are not guided solely by their lower feelings, that all are not infatuated by the word 'Love.' Many who realize that marriage means the devotion of one's entire time to one's family, and consequently the abandonment of all serious study in Literature, Science, and Art, have refused the most tempting offers, and have continued, with zest, in a life of celibacy."

"I have nae met them in Edinbro'," said McWhirter, with interest.

"They are to be met with everywhere," persisted Chapple. "I am continually hearing intellectual women remark that they will never sacrifice their chosen pursuit, their beloved occupation, their prospect of a career, for the mere sake of getting a husband."

"Yes, I agree with you," put in Martell. "I, too, have often met women who seemed so convinced of the truth of the idea, that they were continually impressing it on everybody they met."

Chapple, like most of his countrymen, detested sarcasm, for the reason that he did not understand it.

"Thousands!" he repeated, "thousands! I myself have seen innumerable instances in lady doctors, nurses, post-office clerks, and teachers. Miss Ward, I appeal to you. *You* can give us the names of many such, I have no doubt."

Miss Ward, seeing everybody had turned to her, very properly cast down her eyes. She hesitated just so long as the rules of good society demand from maidens, and then turning to Nina, remarked :

"I can't remember any; can you,

dear, except Edith Rawlinson? She always used to say—didn't she?—that painting put marriage out of the question till——"

"Till Robert Clayton persuaded her she could carry on the two together," said Nina, basely deserting her sex.

"I always think," said Chapple, solemnly, "that an unwedded woman is like some masterpiece fresh from the hand of the master. But married, she is torn away from the environment of genius, and set up where, alas, she may get injured, or defaced, or stained."

This unfortunate ending was rather embarrassing to all present.

"I always think," said Nina, "that an unmarried woman is like an unthreaded needle; one is more struck by her sharpness than by her usefulness."

"For my part I agree with Mr. Chapple," said Patrick, ironically, trying to revenge himself on the blunderer who had put his idol to the blush. "Any modern statue outside its maker's studio is sure to get defaced."

Chapple immediately rose, crossed the room, and insisted on shaking hands with the bewildered Irishman.

"My dear Mr. Weld," said he, "let me congratulate you on having joined the one cause which bands all earnest workers in the nineteenth century together under one flag. It has been reserved for us, my dear sir, to pioneer humanity to the fields where Woman, unfettered, may do exactly what she pleases."

"But if she did," suggested Patrick, "don't you think that there might be a little confusion."

"All great movements are accompanied with confusion," said Chapple; "in fact, I should look with suspicion on any that were not. Confusion must come first, and I can assure you our movement is spreading it everywhere."

"It has nae yet reached Edinbro'," said McWhirter, waking up, and producing a note-book. "Perhaps you could gi' me the parteeculars, Mr. Chapple."

"Certainly!" replied the latter, charmed at the interest his remarks were exciting. "Certainly. Our organ, *The Woman's Cry*, is spreading the movement east and west, and south and north. It has penetrated to nearly every centre of intellectual life. I am surprised to hear you say it has not yet reached your renowned Scottish metropolis, Mr. McWhirter. We have a branch there presided over by Mrs. Fitz-Eustace Macintosh, a woman of the most extraordinary gifts, and a great poetess. I am sorry to say though, that the whole of the British Press (except her countrymen's) and the London publishers have entered into a conspiracy to ignore her for some reason or other."

"Doubtless, as you say, for *some* reason or other," echoed Lofthouse.

Martell was getting rather annoyed that so little notice was taken of him. Usually he had it his own way, but Patrick's paper rendered rather out of place the gloomy paradoxes he was accustomed to be applauded for.

"My publisher tells me," he began, "that he has published twenty-nine books of poetry by women, since he began business, and three cookery books."

"A gourmand says somewhere," said Nina, "that a cook, like a soldier, has to stand the glare of a searching fire, and the smoke that is baneful to the complexion. Every day is a fighting day, but her warfare is almost always without glory!' Think of the fortitude of a woman who cooks her husband's dinner!"

"What of the fortitude of the man that eats it!" said the Socialist.

"But I heard you say yourself, Mr. Martell," said Miss Ward, "that you thought the conversation of most men very dull."

"Teach us the art of scandal, and piquancy will follow," he replied.

Chapple shook his head in sorrow. "Ah," he cried, "turn to woman for charity! If you would only listen to her she would teach you how easy a thing forgiveness is, if——"

"If you may deplore in confidence to some one else the sins of the person you have forgiven!" put in Martell.

"Many a harsh word would remain unspoken," continued Chapple, "if——"

"If one were free to indulge afterwards in a little harmless laughter with one's friends!"

"My dear fellow, you overdo your sarcasm," protested Lofthouse. "You will agree with Chapple that nearly all the bores you meet are men."

"And whose fault is that but woman's?" said the Socialist. "If she would only let him into the secret that there is no warfare between the sexes, but only between members of the same sex, he would cease tiresome flattery of a face where in nine cases out of ten the recipient, but too well aware of the truth, dreads lurking sarcasm above all things. He really only wants a little taking in hand to appreciate the value of a woman's innuendo, and enjoy the full flavour of feminine repartees."

Martell felt he was going rather far; but he was used as a Socialist to never going back.

"At one stroke men would cease to be bores," he explained, "if they were only told that perpetually insisting on making their meaning clear is horribly irritating to a sex that never means what it says."

"Oh, Mr. Martell, they sometimes mean what they say!" cried Miss Ward, struck with sudden horror at the idea that the company might reverse all the maidenly sentiments she had expressed that evening.

"They know at least how to take a hint," admitted Martell, growing cooler. "You have taught me, Miss Ward, that in arguing with a woman success is defeat."

"Victory over a woman in anything is defeat," cried the Poet, impetuously, adding in a whisper to Patrick, "How often poor Chapple has wished to be defeated!"

"Why should we ever wish to cross swords," asked Brinton, who had sat a silent listener most of the time, "when we have the more equal contest of woman fencing woman. I always fancy I see the flash of rapiers when two rivals meet. Each is on guard, brilliant flashes of wit mark the attack, quiet replies the defence, and silence for an instant tells when one has been wounded."

" Mr. Martell would say," said Nina, entering into the spirit of the comparison, " that every woman carries a dagger. She may seem vanquished, but the next instant, a stab tells the bystander that she is not disarmed."

" Ah ! You allow then that women hate one another," cried the Socialist, thinking he saw an opening.

" That must be a virtue in your eyes, if all you say about us be true," laughed Nina.

Martell paid the obvious compliment, and Nina and he stepped on to the balcony, leaving Patrick to the mercies of Miss Ward.

His dissatisfaction was not diminished by hearing shortly afterwards his name mentioned by Martell with a burst of laughter, in which Nina joined. He at once flew to the conclusion that they were laughing at him, and the reflection that he was very mean to suspect it made him more and more irritated. When lovers are not uttering to themselves the platitudes of love, they are thinking the paradoxes of jealousy; and Patrick was not cool-headed enough to see that though Martell was in love, he was in love with himself. He began to respond so baldly to Miss Ward's queries as to his exact views of Froebel's Kindergarten system that she turned to Lofthouse.

"Now, Mr. Lofthouse, you will not refuse us one of your poems?"

Lofthouse protested.

"Oh, how late it has grown! I must be getting home at once. Mr. Lofthouse, you surely will not refuse!"

Lofthouse entreated.

"Oh, but indeed you cannot, Mr. Lofthouse, for you have *promised*."

"Oh, let him off, let him off!" said

Martell, cheerfully, stepping off the
balcony with Nina.

"Aye, let the laddie aff, puir creeture!
Dinna mind the poetry!" said Mc-
Whirter, putting in his spoke.

"Oh, it doesn't matter!" said the
Poet, very quickly. And he repeated the
following lines:

" *'Midst houses dark, frowning in gloomy
      height,*
A tavern through its open doors throws light;
Within, burst after burst the laughter leaps,
Without, a woman in the darkness weeps.

Dost weep that when he struck thee he forgot
The days that till thou diest thou can'st not?
Or has some face brought memory to thy heart
To whisper what thou wast and what thou art?

Some pity and all pass; one looks behind,
While still the laughter floats upon the wind,
One turns the streaming tavern light to see.
In shadow weeps the woman bitterly."

"His poem brought me back to the

realities of life," said Nina, thoughtfully to Patrick, as the two left the Club, and climbed on to the top of a road-car. "How artificial we were to-night! I have never been to such a light-hearted meeting before."

But Patrick was anything but light-hearted. He had fancied that Nina had hinted to Martell that she preferred him to see her home, but that the Socialist had misunderstood her. The simplicity and open-heartedness that made the Irishman so popular among his friends, gave him also all the petulance of a child when crossed.

"What is Mr. Martell by profession?" he inquired, after a short silence.

"He spends most of his time in going about the country, lecturing on Socialism."

"Doesn't he find that very dull?"

"Oh, no. He told me that the constant variety, the new faces, miners in

4*

the North, labourers in the South of England, fascinate him. You really must get to know him better, Patrick, he is such a great friend of mine."

The unlucky phrase "great friend of mine" irritated Patrick still more.

"Yes, he seems to be a great friend of yours. He was, as you predicted, much amused with me," he said, remembering the laugh on the balcony.

"Yes, he was," said Nina, who was growing sleepy, and had not seen what he was driving at. "He told me he was much amused with you."

She meant this as a compliment. Martell had in reality told her that he was much entertained by the paper "In Defence of Woman."

But this was the last straw to Patrick. He could restrain his childish vexation no longer, and burst out:

"Oh, and you laughed with him at me, Nina! You said that we should meet as friends to-night, and now you, you—— "

" Patrick!" said Nina, softly. She was perfectly amazed by the outburst, and much hurt that he should have suspected her of laughing at him with anybody, especially with Martell, the last person in the world.

" Yes," said Patrick, refusing to accept any excuse for the cruel manner in which he thought she had treated him ; " you seem to have forgotten how long we have known each other ; and now—now I never want to go to the Club again!"

Immediately after he had said what was in his mind he felt much relieved, and, like a child, peeped anxiously out of his eyes to see what would happen next.

" Really, Patrick, really, how—" said Nina, in a voice which showed a mixture of just indignation, and an aching heart. She could not bear this quarrel which was so suddenly thrust upon her.

" How what ? " he asked, in a mild voice, quite ready to make concessions, and half sorry, half glad that he had made her wretched.

" How can you be so ridiculous ! " retorted Nina, who began to see exactly what had caused his anger.

" Oh, very well ! " said Patrick, quite defiant again, and with his suspicions rushing back, although a small voice was whispering that he was making a perfect fool of himself.

" We shall soon be home now," said Nina, coldly, and anxious to punish him.

They left the road-car, and walked on in silence for some minutes. Then they began to talk earnestly of things that neither of them took the slightest interest in. The names of some old friends were mentioned.

" Nelly Erskine ! Oh, yes ; I still correspond with her," said Nina. " But I never can feel the same with her as I used to. You know she behaved very coldly to her brother in trouble, and we quarrelled over it. I never feel just the same with people I quarrel with."

"Don't you?" said Patrick, with a sinking heart.

"No," she replied, calmly. "I never do. I daresay it is some fault in my nature; in fact, I am sure it is, for one ought to forget as well as forgive. But somehow or other, and most of all when I'm in the wrong, I never feel as though we were the same. Something happens you know between friends, and they quarrel and that is the end of the friend-ship. There you have the matter in a nut-shell."

"Good-night," she said to Patrick, as she inserted her latch-key. "Good-night, we shall meet, I hope, at the club next week."

Patrick walked home with a heavy heart. He said to himself that they

could never feel the same exactly towards one another, and he reproached
himself over and over again for having
behaved so badly,

" What a fool I have made of myself
this evening ! " he finally confided to
his pillow, when he at length fell asleep.

WHICH LEADS TO SOCIALISM.

III.

WHICH LEADS TO SOCIALISM.

WHEN Patrick awoke the next morning, his folly had assumed large proportions. "How very contemptible I must have seemed," he thought; and he kept asking himself how contemptible. At one moment he called himself, "Ass!" at the next, "Idiot!" At dinner he grew more cheerful, and fancied Nina must have forgotten all about the incident; but by nightfall he concluded that she had meant what she said, and that he could never be the same to her again. Then he said that she had only meant to frighten him, or to make fun of him. But the next moment something whispered, "Her

voice showed that all was over between
you." Several times he sat down to
write to her, but after reading the few
stammering lines, his heart failed him,
and he tore the letters up, and flung
them away. A thousand times he told
himself indignantly that if he had been
contemptible before, he was far more
contemptible now to think so much of a
trifle ; but hard words did not do much
for him, and he always returned to the
question, "What if I never am the same
to her again ? " Besides all this, his brain
was busy with two important points :
first, did Nina care for Martell? secondly,
did Martell love Nina ? And the bitter
reflection that he might have been right
in his suspicions after all, did not lessen
his perplexity.

His conduct may convince the reader,
who knows lovers well in theory, that
that Patrick was an unnaturally weak,
foolish, and unmanly young Irishman,

but let him remember that the epithets
he chooses to apply to the unfortunate
young fellow, may not please other
readers who have put love into practice.
Patrick was, in truth, deeply in love, and
his one wish was to see Nina and make
it up. Should he be so lucky as to be
forgiven, he swore to himself that he
wished he might never see her again, if
he ever behaved badly to her, his whole
life long. Never had he passed such a
lingering week; but at length the club-
night arrived, and he hastened away to
Ivy Lane. He was decidedly early, but
curiously enough he encountered Nina,
who was gazing into a shop-window.

"What a beautiful night!" she remarked in a voice that a lover with the
utmost desire to make himself miserable,
could hardly describe as cold.

As it was so early, they paced up and
down the narrow street, curved like a
half-moon.

Now that he was actually with her again, his tongue refused to speak the words he had been preparing for the last forty-eight hours.

"Nina," he began, " I—I——"

"Look at that boy up there!" said Nina, rather quickly, pointing to a window where a boy sat reading, his head resting on his hand, with a tall candle beside him. The light fell on his fair flushed face, eagerly devouring the pages. A woman's voice called " Tom !" but the boy read on. Then as she called again, he looked round alarmed, shut the book up, and blew the light out softly. Presently a woman walked across the now dark room, put her head out as though expecting to see her son hanging from the bars, and remarking, " Why, he isn't there after all !" went away.

Patrick felt that now or never was the time, and he burst out before Nina had time to interrupt the confession she was nervously anticipating, " Nina, I want to tell you that—that I think—I hope you——"

" Patrick !" she broke in hurriedly, "You know we have always been friends. Don't let us now be foolish, and——"

Their hands met in the dark, and Patrick felt that her touch lifted a mountain from his heart.

"'Tis a braw nicht !" said McWhirter's voice close beside them ; and Patrick cursed the unhappy Scotchman, who had robbed him of such an opportunity.

The three turned into the Club, where McWhirter did not improve the situation by drawing Nina into a corner and making her give her opinion on a packet of the photographs of his relatives, which he produced from his coat-tail pocket.

At length Martell arrived, and read with studied indifference as follows :—

"My paper this evening is but a collection of fragmentary thoughts carelessly thrown together. The only thread, as you will see, that runs throughout is contempt for the existing order of things, and a loose advocacy of Socialism. You will remember that I have explained scientific Socialism as I understand it, on past occasions.

"The ordinary merchant looks with intense aversion on begging and stealing, though his trade is but a combination of the two cemented with industry. His life is passed in begging the world to take his goods; his success is insured in successful cheating, or as he prefers to call it, 'having the best of the bargain.' To this end he employs a number of 'travellers,' who are paid according to their skill in persuading men to take more than they can possibly sell of goods which are not what they are represented to be. This, we are told, is 'the custom of the trade,' a phrase which is as elastic as the consciences of the men who employ it. With this phrase, the manufacturer swindles the merchant, the merchant the tradesman, the tradesman the public, and the public one another. Nobody objects, for all are guilty. When the wheel is set rolling, how can a spoke refuse to follow? When a spoke in a carriage-wheel breaks, the smith replaces it by a new one; but we have improved on that, we mend it, and whitewash it in the Bankruptcy Court, and give it another trial. One virtue trade has, and that is a great one; it offers our sons a safe career. In apprenticing a boy to the most humdrum business, we can guarantee his future, provided he is fairly dishonest. Before I have done with trade, I would give its followers two pieces of advice. First, when you are forced to engage a man at starvation wages, it is cruelty to deprive him of soft words. Second, in selling your soul to the devil, do not, as so many eminent merchants have done in working themselves night and day, part with your body: it is a ruinous system of discount for cash.

"Do not think, however, that I rate the business man lower than the thief. The State gains more by the former, for while the gain of the burglar is pretty sure to find its way to the publican, the dishonest gain of the manufacturer occasionally goes at his death to build a reformatory. A thief's apprentices end on the gallows, or at the best draw a good deal of money from our pockets for lodging in a well-built, well-drained, well-ventilated, and well-lighted palace, whereas the younger sons of merchants not infrequently take a literary turn, or go into the Church. Thieving has indeed many drawbacks. For one thing, it promotes class hatred. Competition is nowadays so keen that it is not extraordinary a merchant should detest a thief when the latter steals in a single night what the former has taken a year to filch.   For another thing, a thief's business is often connected with bloodshed.   Were it not for this fatal flaw, Society might class him as high as a bank director, a publisher, or even place him on an equality with a member of the Stock Exchange.   But the English never pardon the conjunction of failure and bloodshed.   You ask, then, why has not a certain eminent statesman been hanged long ago? My answer is that whereas this eminent statesman shed blood in the Soudan Campaign, his General was responsible for *the failure*, and as each was clearly responsible for only one crime, both were rewarded.

"Another objection to the thief's occupation is that exigencies require him to be constantly moving. Could he only change his name, and select a locality where people would be sure of

5

finding him at home, he would be as
respectable a member of society as
Dodson or Fogg of Lincoln's Inn.
This prejudice in the English mind
against shifting the scene of action has,
till comparatively lately, proved fatal to
the player, and he has been classed as
a vagabond in every hum-drum head.
But directly the stroller exchanged his
theatre of wood for one of stone, the
laws that forbade him contaminating the
souls of the citizens were exchanged
for others that permitted him to
burn their bodies alive, and the magis-
trate who would formerly have committed him to prison, was anxious to be
invited to supper.

" Beggars and thieves are always
coupled together, but, to my mind, with
much injustice. So long as the one keeps
out of the workhouse, and the other out
of the prison, Society gives them picturesque names and pronounces them in-

teresting ; but now that 'brigand' and
'mendicant' are out of fashion, our
statesmen erect poorhouses and Bride-
wells, and strive to make it equally
degrading to enter either. In this they
have never quite succeeded. While the
honest poor steadily refuse to camp out
in the casual ward, public opinion,
despite official platitudes, refuses to
believe that he who asks for bread and
is given a stone is on a par with him,
who, aided by a dark turn in the lane,
exchanges a stone for bread—for the
blood that stains the flint is not the
thief's.

"Another point in favour of the beggar
is that from the individualist's point of
view, no class is freer from the vice of
demanding State aid. This trait, indeed,
is strongly marked from his earliest
childhood. No State education for him,
no State inspection, none of that enerva-
ting control, which according to our

greatest living philosopher is so baneful to our national life! Begging, in
short, offers a wide field to the able. I
submit that there are good openings in
the profession for young men who are
too scrupulous to go into business, too
lazy to become clerks, and not courage-
ous enough to turn authors. It is true
that to beg is thought degrading by
manufacturers who give starvation wages,
but then it is also thought to be
humiliating by clerks who dare not
condemn their master's dishonesty, and
it is said not to pay by journalists! But
does it pay? From the statistics avail-
able there seems no doubt that the
average beggar — ranging from the
match-box beggar to the writer of the
begging letter—earns over double the
weekly wage of the seamstress of East
London, who works twelve hours a day;
and a little more than a writer in the
Civil Service, who draws £75 a year.

Be it understood that we urge only the able to take up the profession. It is only the extreme delicacy of touch required for success that keeps the ill-paid clerk and dissatisfied mechanic from rushing into the business. As it is we should strongly advise no tyro to enter who will not be content with £65 per annum for the first two years, but it may be added that it is a profession in which money can be saved, and when a little capital has been accumulated a man can leave begging behind, and climb to a higher stage of society where 'soliciting' takes its place. Finally, three objections may be disposed of. Some authorities say, 'Once a beggar, always a beggar.' If this be so, which we deny, it is gratifying to think, from our experience of our friends that so many people are settled for life in a not unprofitable industry. Secondly, it is said that begging involves a course of

unblushing deceit, but we answer that a
false leg is no more necessary to a man
who enters the trade, than is the truth
to an advertiser. Thirdly, it is objected
that if mendicancy be made a recognized
profession there will be a tremendous cry
of 'Competition!' Let our tyro, however, walk the streets in a frock coat
and a silk hat, and it will be hard to
distinguish him from any other respectable thief.

"I will now conclude my remarks,"
continued Martell, "with a few words
on Socialism." Thus speaking he
plunged into his beloved subject. All
his calmness was gone, all his logic was
lost, swept away by his own eloquence.
Nature seemed to have revenged herself
for his indifference to everything else
natural or the reverse, by making him
ridiculous on this hobby of Socialism.
It looked as though he had bottled up
all the indignation that he had felt on

other subjects, for the support of this most theoretical of theories. Forgetting he was speaking to a dilettanti Club, and not to the Northern miners he thundered :—

[1] " ' Proletariat production—capitalist appropriation : workers make—traders take. Socialized production : individual exchange. Work in concert : exchange at war. Supremacy of town : subservience of country. Over-crowded cities : empty fields. Such are the briefest possible statements of the economical and social forces which result in our present anarchy, not for one class alone, though that suffers far the most, but for all. Capital dominates the planet, acts irrespectively of all nationalities, grabs its profits irrespective of all creeds and conditions : capital is international, un-

[1] With apologies to the joint authors of " A Summary of the Principles of Socialism."

sectarian, destitute of regard for humanity or religion.

"'Even the middle-class debating club at Westminster, which passes muster as the English House of Commons, has found itself compelled by the exigencies of the case to interpose between the employers and their wage-slaves, between the Irish landlords and their serfs, between adulterating poisoners and their victims. Yet the House of Commons must go. Its death will be that of the House of Lords. Violence! But let us be careful of what comes after, for remember that in the case of the French proletariat, when the war was over Paris found that though she had got rid of the Emperor with his gang of professional gamblers and prostitutes, France was to be handed to the exploitation of a reactionist Republic. Let us therefore be cautious. Let us be moderate! Our demands are at present small. We ask first of all for the land. Though one does not see exactly how the over-worked hinds of England are solely to undertake the agricultural management of the country, still that is no reason why a handful of persons should draw vast revenues from a monopoly fraudulently seized from their countrymen ; still less why the land in towns, and the minerals below the land in country should be held for the benefit of the few.

" 'But Socialists have no factious prejudices, and are influenced by no jealousies of a clique. We call therefore also for the immediate management and ownership of the railways by the State, so that the inland communications of the country may be under the control of the people at large, and carried on for their benefit, regard being had to the full remuneration of the labour of all who are engaged in the work of transport.

5*

" 'As with railways so with shipping. There the whole economical forms are ready, in the same way, for immediate management by the State, and the transfer could be arranged almost without a hitch.

" 'This is borne out by the greatest scientists in despite of huckster economy and huckster economists, whose principal professors are forced to eat their own words as administrators and to stultify their teaching as thinkers by sheer pressure of the course of events. At this hour the State is by far the largest employer of labour in the kingdom. But I have said enough to show you that if the proletariat of the world unite, they will conquer the Capitalists, and the Bourgeoisie, the two greatest foes of Humanity. Unite! only unite.

" 'For this we educate, to this end we agitate, to achieve a certain victory for all we organize. Unite! Unite! Unite!'"

For half an hour longer he continued in this strain, while Patrick sat aghast at the cataract; though he rejoiced in his heart at the sudden revelation of Martell's craze. " Capitalist," " proletariat," " bourgeoisie," " labour-force," " hind," " drudge," " organization," " coterie," " bed rock," " marauder," " altruism," " surplus value," " universal brotherhood," " propaganda," " primeval man," " landlord rascality," " fuglemen," " bare subsistence," " monopoly," " wage slave class," " class robbery," " countless generations," and " exploitation," throbbed through his brain till he feebly wondered whether he was bourgeois or proletariat, or merely an overworked hind exploited by his capitalistic and marauding employer. Finally, he gave up his vain efforts to reach the bed-rock of the matter, and he sat hopeless and dazed, not daring to laugh lest Nina should think him ill-natured.

At length the Socialist brought his harangue to a close. With the final word "municipalisation" he threw his papers into the firegrate.

Miss Ward was always delighted with lectures she did not understand, for she rightly thought they must be exceptionally intellectual.

"I should like to say," she began, "that my experiences are very different to Mr. Martell's. There is much distress, but then the poor *are* so wasteful. Several women I know burn coal. Now we always use coke at home. And I am told the men smoke a great deal of bad tobacco, and injure their digestions. Would it not be more sensible if they bought a little of the very best? And then they *are* so proud. My brother tells me that they will not move into the model dwellings, because they dislike showing certificates of character."

"Ah, how truly wicked, how foolish!" murmured Chapple.

"Yes," she continued, delighted at his remark. "Don't you think, Mr. Chapple, it is very sad? Only a week ago a woman was most impertinent to a dear friend of mine, who, asking her to allow the baby to be christened, said, 'You know, Mrs. Thomas, we must not have any little heathens in Cornwall Buildings!'"

"Most preposterous in the extreme!" cried Chapple, indignant at such unfeminine pride.

This exhibition roused Brinton, who immediately attacked Martell on English Socialism.

"Your denunciation of trade and business men is absurd," said he. "Of course the merchant carries his private faults into business life, just as the clerk or your favourite 'proletariat' carry theirs. Perhaps he underpays them, and perhaps they waste their time. What then? But it is characteristically mean of the clerk to decry the man on whom he depends. You talk of merchants and manufacturers as though they should all have been strangled at the hour of their birth. I, as you know, have been a working man, and no cant is so sickening to me as the cant of the working classes. They slander their employers for doing what they themselves are longing to do; but without them, or men like them, they would hardly get bread to eat. They are envious of the man who has risen, either by industry, or talent, or pluck; the man who bears all the battle, who takes everything on his shoulders, and pays his subordinates what they are worth."

"Do you not think, Mr. Chapple," sighed Miss Ward, "that the spectacle of the relations of employer to employed in England is very unedifying?"

"An unfit survival," replied Chapple, "is always truly barbarian beside the complexus of civilization—socialized man."

"Perhaps you will give us your experience of the Socialists, Brinton," sneered Martell.

"Nearly all the Socialists I ever met," continued Brinton, "were blind optimists. Analyse their speeches, and you find nothing, simply nothing but a denunciation of existing evils, and a glowing picture of the ideal State, the way to attain to which they leave to the inflamed imaginations of their hearers, who generally conclude that the way to Utopia is to march along in a street procession with red flags."

"It is very characteristic of the *bourgeoisie*," said Martell, ironically, "to ignore scientific Socialism and Karl Marx."

"I am coming to them," replied Brinton, roused for once. "Socialistic leaders are of one of two classes, the hot and the cold. The hot draw their adherents from the poor, who will shout, and no wonder, poor fellows! for anybody who promises them a bit of bread, and to whom the offer of a whole slice, spread with Socialistic butter, is simply irresistible. The cold adherents are those who sit contentedly down to prepare flawless systems of government for a people that is a mass of contradictions, men who cheerfully contribute their pence to the propaganda of an Utopia that is rendered impossible by an European war, or a rise in the price of wheat. These two parties, who once wrote, 'Socialists are influenced by no jealousies of a clique,' have quarrelled over the important question whether there is more chance of converting the universe to their views by a system of halfpenny leaflets, or by concentrating their strength, and getting a representative into the House of Commons. The contempt that these two sections have for one another shows, it is true, on each

side a certain amount of shrewdness.
But the utmost that the hot party can do
is to turn themselves into Radicals ; and
the utmost the cold can do is to produce
a masterpiece of theory, which will be
triumphantly picked to pieces twenty
years after it has been forgotten, as was
the case with ' Das Kapital.' "

" Your acquaintance with English
Socialism," said Martell, who looked
highly amused, " is sufficient to enable
you to give us a lively caricature of the
two sections ; but your talent for super-
ficiality will hardly lead you to ignore
the fact that the whole tendency of our
legislation is Socialistic, that the Labour
party and the trade unionists are joining
hands all over the country, and that
hundreds of intellectual men have been
converted in the last few months to our
side."

" Thirty years ago," replied Brinton,
" the pendulum swung towards in-

dividualism. Now it is nearing Socialism. Do you really believe it will
not swing back again? It is true
that there is now a tendency towards
Socialism; it is true that the examples set
by Germany and America are arguments
in your favour; but what will be the net
results of your success? You say happiness for the people. I say no, and only
time can decide. Your movement is as
ephemeral as any other. I contend that
there is no deep desire in human nature
for Socialism, but the exact contrary;
and I say that Socialism is far and away
too rigid to satisfy any people for long.
You are in reality misled by the merely
temporary attraction it has for mankind.
But your Socialism can never get far;
for directly it gains the Radicals it be-
comes Opportunist, and Opportunism is
fatal to its vital principle. After all,
your aim is to force people to do what
Christians teach should be done through

kindness.   Will you succeed better than they ? "

Brinton stopped his harangue at last, feeling that he was talking of what he knew very little, and of what Martell knew less.

" Yes, we shall succeed better," answered the Socialist, "because being forced to do a thing saves people the trouble of perpetually keeping themselves up to the mark.   How much cash would the State get if the payment of taxes was voluntary ?   Morality will be the income-tax of the Socialists."

" Yes, and the only way you can come into power is by promising to repeal both," retorted Brinton.   " But your idea of a co-operative commonwealth is simply ludicrous," he continued.   " Look at London !   Its inhabitants are split up into clusters of stars circling round thousands of suns, represented by the trades, the professions, the ablest and the richest men, the capitalists, the———"

" Public-houses ! " suggested Patrick.

" Exactly. Well, without these suns we Londoners would find ourselves in the dark."

" These capitalistic suns of yours often suffer eclipse," said Martell.

"They are often eclipsed by fresh suns," said Brinton, "the warmth and wealth of which is created by the shattering of many humble stars. The principle of this universe of London is employment, and naturally there are a good many collisions in the rush of competition."

"What we Socialists want to do," explained Martell, "is to exchange this astronomical muddle for a solar system. We would crush all your individual suns into one huge sun, the State, round which the planets—Mars the army, Mercury literature, Jupiter the law—would circle harmoniously."

" I should circle round Venus," murmured Patrick to himself, glancing in Nina's direction.

But Nina had disappeared into the balcony some time before with Chapple, and the sound of their earnest voices came indistinctly through the window.

"No, Mr. Chapple," Lofthouse, who was sitting nearest, heard her say, " it can never be."

" But I ask—— " said Chapple's voice. The remainder was lost to the listener.

" I wonder what on earth they can be saying," thought the Poet. " I wouldn't answer for Chapple when he is left alone in the moonshine with a pretty girl. It always turns his brain. Still, it's none of my business. I won't listen any more."

"I assure you, Mr. Chapple, you are mistaken," came Nina's voice again, in remarkably decided tones.

" Good gracious, I believe it's a pro-

posal ! " thought Lofthouse, half in
doubt. " Martell was right when he
said nothing is so dangerous to a man
as a warm June night." He left the
window and joined the others, who
were yawning, and had not recovered
yet from the dose of Socialism.

" You always come so appropriately,
Mr. Lofthouse," simpered Miss Ward.
" Only fancy ! we were wishing that
you would recite one of your beautiful
poems."

The poet had already selected the
one he intended to repeat that evening,
but he had calculated on Nina being
present. " Chapple, too," he thought,
" would have liked to have heard it.
He has good taste, though he is such an
ass." He waited for a moment in the
hope that they would leave the balcony,
but they remained there, and were still
talking earnestly.

The happy thought struck the poet

that he could repeat his verses to Nina
alone afterwards, and feeling mollified
by Miss Ward's judicious use of her
adjectives, he began :

" *The primrose peeps through the bracken dry,*
Clouds chase clouds across the sky ;
The ash-poles, slender and silver, sway
On the hillside, in the morning grey.

Sweet is the song that the wind sings to me:
  ' Your Love is waiting, waiting.
The apple will fall, but a touch needs the tree ;
  Your Love is waiting, waiting.'
Her curls are tangled, tangled by the wind ;
  Her cheeks are fresher, fresher than the rain.
The grasses at her bosom quiver, rise and fall,
  Quiver as she draws her breath to fall again.

The mist rolls up to the stone wall low ;
'Neath the hawthorn hedge no wind doth blow.
Sway, oh, ash-poles slender ! oh rain, pelt on !
Her eyes bring the sunshine, though no sun has
  shone.

Oh, sweet is the song that the wind sings to me:
  ' Your Love is waiting, waiting.
The bracken is dry 'neath the hawthorn tree ;
  Your Love is waiting, waiting.' "

"It reminds me faintly of one of Meredith's, Mr. Lofthouse," said a voice, and the poet, looking up, saw that Chapple and Nina had just stepped back into the room.

"I believe she only heard half of it!" said Lofthouse to himself, with some vexation; but he speedily forgot his annoyance in wondering whether Nina's rather subdued manner, and Chapple's bewildered air, meant that a proposal had been made and rejected. Evidently none of the others noticed anything out of the common, though perhaps the discussion at the other end of the room was demanding all their attention.

"He does well to make verses on the country," Martell remarked. "He would find it difficult to take London for his theme, the city 'where men and women, half-clothed and half-fed, stumble from a pauper cradle to a pauper grave!'"

"Good gracious, Mr. Martell!" cried Miss Ward.

"I was only quoting William Morris again," he returned; "but speaking seriously, you can count the beauties of London on the fingers of one hand."

"London is inexhaustible," cried Lofthouse, "quite inexhaustible! Wherever I go I see fresh beauties, fresh vistas, fresh——"

"Advertisements!" suggested Nina, recovering her equanimity.

"Advertisements educate the people," put in McWhirter, "which is most important. I assure you, Miss Lindon, the other day I was actually deceived by a monkey on a hoarding, and I tried to stroke it. A very life-like beestie! You know I am a bit shortsighted, and——"

"Hush!" said Miss Ward, in a warning tone, as she saw the poet's eye glaring at the interruption. "Go on, please, Mr. Lofthouse. I am much interested by what you say."

"Well," said Lofthouse, swallowing his

6

wrath, "I say that London is full of beauty,
perfectly full of beauty.   Look at Seven
Dials!   I assure you it is most poetical!
And, indeed, I am writing a little poem on
the subject.   You think I am joking, but I
can assure you that it is to Drury Lane at
midnight that a man should go who would
successfully translate Dante's 'Inferno.'"

"Yes," echoed Patrick, who feared
lest the poet's enthusiasm should make
a good cause ridiculous.   "Why do we
get pictures year after year of scenes in
Venice, and not one of Wentworth
Street (now that Petticoat Lane has
been so barbarously treated) on a Sunday morning?"

"I went down Wentworth Street last
May," said the Poet, "and saw a mass
of colour as brilliant as the gleaming
mackerel the hawkers were crying.   Hundreds of women with pink, or buttercup
yellow, or olive green, or dark blue shawls
thrown over their heads, Jewesses with

dark brown hair, Irishwomen with those
exquisite deep blue eyes and black eye-
brows, were sitting in the doorways, or
standing at the stalls, bearing the chaff
of the men good-humouredly.   Oh, the
colour in those piles of blood oranges !
The road was choked with fish, fruit,
flowers, vegetables, and meat, and
in the middle two streams of men and
women struggled to pass one another,
jostling to right and left.   At the top
of the street I found a little recess,
where a ring of black-eyed girls were
dancing and singing :

"Oh, Jenny is a-weeping, a-weeping, a-weeping ;
Oh, Jenny is a-weeping on a fine summer's
 day."

" You are not really enthusiastic over
the picturesque, you're enthusiastic over
the women," remarked Martell.   " But
how on earth you can draw such a picture of Petticoat Lane, I don't know.

Where I only see the vilest, the most
degraded faces, faces yellow with disease
and stained with crime, you find form
and colour, and light and shade, and
goodness knows what. I do not know
which is the most repulsive, the eyes of
the wrinkled hags one meets there,
greedy with the love of gain, or the eyes
of the men brutal with cold lust."

" Pray remember, Mr. Martell," interrupted Chapple, "that we have been
honoured with the presence of our *lady*
friends this evening."

"Well, how you can extract from a
street of the most repulsive Jews, the
most brutalized men, and the most degraded women, the glorious flashes of
colour you describe, is astounding!"

" Colour!" said Lofthouse, scornfully,
" colour there was on this day, but the
man who looks for colour in London is
a fool. Who wants colour when you
have such exquisite light and shade? I

really believe, Martell, you know very
little of London."

"Indeed!" cried the Socialist, who
prided himself on being indifferent to
any attack on his person, his virtues, or
his creed, but whose foible was his
knowledge, for on that he built his
theories.

"Yes, as little of its beauties as the
cabman who has driven over every inch.
Do you know the fortress of Lower
Thames Street?"

"Or the silence of Hosier Lane?"
said Patrick.

"Have you ever passed through West
Smithfield on an April day, with the
blue sky and the fleecy white moun-
tains of cloud overhead, and the racing
shadows contrasting with the sunshine
on the redbrick of the market?"

"Or through the ravine of the
Minories?" asked Patrick.

"Have you ever seen the Scotchmen

dance the Highland fling over the naked swords in the heart-shaped ring to the skirl of the bagpipes?" demanded Loft-house.

"And where and when may that Exhibition be seen?" asked Martell, contemptuously.

"Ah, you may weel call it an Exhibition," interrupted McWhirter, who had as usual missed the point in note-taking; "and a most intellectual exhibition, too, I can testify, having seen it myself in Flower and Dean Street on Easter morning."

"I trust that no women are present at such an insane diversion," said Chapple, sententiously.

"Eh, but there are," chuckled McWhirter; "and you should see the lasses stroke the laddies' bare calves."

"Disgraceful! how unwomanly!" murmured Miss Ward. "How can they be so utterly lost to all sense of decency? Ah, Mr. Chapple, no wonder the tone of the East End is so low!"

" The fact is, Lofthouse," said the Socialist, "that as you have an artistic bent, and as you are kept in London all the year round, you translate the things that are utterly ugly in themselves into things of beauty merely for your own satisfaction. We shall hear you next calling the Regent's Canal a fairy stream, and Maida Vale a smiling valley."

" The fact is," cried Lofthouse, who generally grew paradoxical in argument, " that the rich never know the best parts of London at all.   How can they, when they rarely approach the Thames below Richmond ?   Pall Mall is mediocre by day, and South Kensington is tame by night."

" Eh, but the Ceety ! " began Mc-Whirter.   " I'm thinkin' you'll nae persuade the laddies to admire the asphalte, Mr. Lofthouse, or the braw hansom cabs, Hoot mon, but they make a fearsome din ! "

"Refute him, Lofthouse," cried Patrick; "you have an easy task."

"Give us a little lecture on the subject," suggested the Socialist, ironically.

"I will," cried Lofthouse, taking up the challenge. "Why, this very house is in the midst of the most suggestive bit of London. Turn into 'Duke's Head Passage,' opposite, on an April day, and listen to the caged linnet singing to the strip of blue sky shut in by the overhanging, almost touching, houses. Then comes a shower, and drives the gossiping clerks and the 'odd men,' and the old woman with her pile of oranges, and her cry, 'Two a penny—all sugar,' under the dark archways, or into the dairy, with its shining pewter and baskets of cakes, or to the little eating-house, high settles, kippers, and all. They wait till the bright drops trickle in the sunshine down the panes, and the rain water gushes over the cobbles from the spout, before going back to work."

"A clerk's life round here can't be so bad after all," said Nina, thinking of how Patrick spent his days, and trying to extract a grain of comfort from the poet.

"Oh, but they have no idea that but a stone's throw away is the most beautiful sight in Europe—Samuel Butler says so, and he is right—the view of St. Paul's from Fleet Street. I was passing there the other day just after a shower, when the cross of the Cathedral gleamed in the sunshine with wet gold, when every stone and every turret stood out in the quivering air as distinctly as on the day they were chiselled, yet nobody turned their head, or noticed the thunder clouds in flight towards the north."

He subsided suddenly, suspecting that every one of his hearers must be thinking him egotistical, which reflection was indeed short of the truth.

Patrick hastened to the rescue.

6*

"Every district has its charm, whether it be the bustle and life of Islington, the foreign gilt and tawdry splendour of Leicester Square, the haddock-curing of Bethnal Green, the mysteries of Shadwell, the peaceful beauties of Highgate, or——"

"The intrigues of King Street, St. James," remarked Martell, grimly.

His irony was lost on Miss Ward, who declared she had had no idea it was so late. "How quickly the time passes when one is with dear friends, Mr. Chapple!"

"If we indulge in the pleasures of congenial society, Miss Ward," he replied, "we must pay the penalty. But who would not so indulge on such an exquisite night? May I see you home?"

The lady gladly assented, and the two set off together.

"You see even you women, who go in for being independent," said Patrick to Nina, "are only independent within the recognized conventionalities."

" I don't see anything of the sort," said Nina. " When has conventionality prevented me from going anywhere ? "

" Even such a simple thing as staying up to see the sunrise from London Bridge, as we are going to do, is debarred you," said he.

" Who are we ? " she inquired.

" Oh, all of us—Lofthouse, Brinton, Martell, myself, and," he added, sinking his voice, " I am afraid, McWhirter. You see it would be out of the question for you to come."

This assumption nettled Nina extremely.

"I should not hesitate a minute, if——"

" Then why don't you come ? " cried Patrick. " It's all very well in theory, but you see when you come to the point you——"

" I will come," said Nina, a little stiffly.

ON LONDON BRIDGE.

IV.

THE clocks of London were striking twelve when Nina and Patrick passed on to the bridge. Brinton and Lofthouse were standing watching the river from one of the embrasures; McWhirter and Martell were questioning a policeman on the habits of suicides.

It was a dark night, but now and again the moon sailed from behind the clouds, and threw a silver wand along the water. Down the river shone a clear red light, which shot a beam through the darkness till it reached the moonlight; then it faded away, shooting

again over the gloomy water beyond.
The breeze sighed softly as it played
round the arches of the bridge, but
every now and then its sound was lost
in the faint roar which floated over the
water from a point of the horizon where
the sky was reddening with a growing
wave of mellow light. A fire had
broken out in Rotherhithe.

The tide had turned, and was ebbing
past the black houses, rising at the
water's edge, square and grim as prisons ;
past the silent wharves and quays lying
low in shadow ; and, rippling against the
dusky barges chained in a pack in the
middle of the current, the river glided
onward to the sea, flowing sullenly in
shade, but bubbling in a silver torrent
where the moonlight struck the water.

The six members selected a seat on
the east side, and leaning on the parapet
watched the mellow light spreading in
the gloom, till suddenly a tongue of fire

leapt upwards, and the black houses stood out against a crimson sky.

The Socialist stretched his arm towards the flames.

"'Tis some factory burning," he said; "and yonder lie the workers asleep, unconscious of the misfortune which has taken the bread from their mouths. And to how many among the three millions yonder is bread assured beyond the day which is about to break? Thousands of them are utterly destitute, thousands of them are fed by charity, and thousands of them—women—escape that charity, and live by degradation."

His rhetoric exasperated McWhirter, for it had anticipated a burst of eloquence on the wealth of Great Britain, suggested by the dark warehouses lying beneath.

"Tut! you forget the rich," he said, "who have troubles greater than the puir."

"I don't deny," returned Martell, con-

temptuously, " that the diseases brought
on by eating and drinking too much are
a great affliction. I don't deny that an
evil conscience is very terrible to a
sensitive mind—a conscience that is so
nicely educated that it refuses to be
silenced by the charity which its owner
bestows from wealth that is not his own."

" Bide a wee, bide a wee," said
McWhirter, excitedly, "you are forgetting the School Board, I'm thinking, Mr.
Martell. Just a gran' monument to the
inteelectual abilities of those who would
raise the puir bodies a bit higher ! "

" Thank you," said the Socialist,
sarcastically, " the East-enders don't care
to be raised any higher ; they are giddy
enough.   The School Board !   An
improved educating elevator in the
English hotel, bringing up everybody to
the top, and having nothing to do with
the majority who fall back down the
shaft, for there isn't room for many at

the top.   But to bring them up is its duty, and it does it."

" You are very pessimistic to-night !" cried the Poet.

" Mine is but theory," replied Martell, who felt much flattered, " but you should ask Brinton to tell you something of the life of the poor.   I believe he knows."

Brinton was leaning against the parapet, a little way off, his head buried in his hands, but at the mention of his name he came forward.

" I was watching the fire," he said, apologetically.   " It will not burn itself out till the morning.   Does anybody want me ?"

" Yes," said Nina, lightly.   " We are all feeling a little dull and commonplace, Mr. Brinton, and we want you to tell us a story."

Brinton thought for a minute.   Then raising his head, he said in a hard voice, " Well, be it so.   I will tell you some-

thing I once heard that happened at
Chiswick; but remember you must not
blame me if you find it serious."

"The more serious the better," said
Nina; "it will get us into training."
And she leant back in the seat, and the
others settled themselves as comfortably
as they could.

"It will seem like a story out of a
book," said Brinton, "but it is true as
surely as the broad arrow is real that is
cut into the stone at your feet."

He leant his elbows on the parapet,
and, gazing fixedly at the river beneath,
began :—

"One February afternoon a woman
stood looking out on the river from a
garret in Hammersmith. The sun was
setting, a ball of fire sinking into the
marshy fields; and the river hurried by,
black and swollen with the melted
snow.

"The woman, gazing across the water,

saw on the further bank only the yellow
osiers bending in the wind, and the row
of stunted willows against the sky. The
wind blew up stream, and the waves fell
back in anger from its strength, and set
in a cross current towards the shore.
The woman gazing across the water saw
a little boat, with a black figure seated in
it, struggling against the current. The
rower bent to his oars, but his efforts
only served to keep him from being
swept back by the racing water. Nothing human was in sight save this solitary
black figure, which would soon be lost in
the darkness.

"Suddenly there came a knock, and
the woman ran to open the door. Then,
as she recognized the faces of the two
men who entered, she uttered a cry of
dismay, and threw herself on her miserable bed, which was placed in the corner
furthest from the door. The room was
bare save for this bed, and a bundle of

shavings and broken pieces of wood, which lay in a faded lilac apron on the hearth-stone.

" The woman was one of those poor creatures you see in the early morning, waiting for the odds and ends of wood and the sweepings which the warehouses throw into the street; one of those old women who, with backs bowed under sacks of paper, search in the gutter for scraps of cloth to sell, for scraps of food to eat, women who mutter to themselves in the cold, women whose faded rags you avoid touching with your sleeve when you meet them in the dark alleys of the City.

" This woman was a month behind with her rent; she had promised to pay four successive times, and each time had failed to bring the money. She had been sick, but she had concealed the fact, afraid of being driven to the work-house. At last the landlord would wait no longer. Knowing it was useless to summons her, he sent two men to turn her into the street. By a judicious mixture of hard words and promises, they hoped to get her to leave the house.

"But the woman refused to stir from her bed. From her refuge she cursed the men and bade them begone. The law gave them no power to eject her by force, so their perplexity drove them to a last resource—to break the windows and unhinge the door.

"The woman begged and prayed for mercy.

"'Give me a little time!' she cried. 'Only a little time, and I will pay you. Give me a little time to work; one week more. Leave me alone for only one week more!'

"But they did not heed her, and they broke three panes out of four, thinking the cold would drive her to the workhouse,

"'Now for the door, mate!' said one to the other.

"'Oh, my God! Give me a little time!' cried the woman from the bed, 'and I will work and pay you.'

"'Let the damned thing be, Jack,' said the other man, roughly.

"'If you want to get the bullet, I don't,' answered Jack, and he began to unscrew the hinges.

"'Oh, God in heaven, have mercy!' cried the old woman. 'I'm perishing with the cold.'

"'Stash it up, Jack,' said the man. 'I'm sick of the job!' With difficulty he persuaded his companion to leave the door alone; and the two went downstairs together.

"When they had got into the street, the man who had shown a little pity, found he had left his chisel behind. His comrade stopped to light his pipe, and said that he would wait below, while the other ran to fetch the tool.

"The man reascended the creaking wooden staircase, and opened the door again."

Brinton paused for a second, as though he saw before him what he was describing.

"He saw the three broken panes of glass with their jagged edges; and his chisel lying on the floor, the light glancing on the steel from the window above. He saw the discoloured wall-paper rising and falling as the wind passed between it and the wall; the spark of fire in the grate, and the bundle of shavings lying on the hearth-stone.

"The woman lay on the bed of rags with her face turned towards the wall. She had not moved since the men had left her; she had not spoken, nor uttered a sound.

"He approached the window, and looking out saw the sun had almost set. The river ran on, a mass of black and

7

angry water, and all colour had faded
from the osier-beds, and the row of willows.   The little boat was still in sight ;
it had crept a little further, and the solitary rower was still labouring at his oars,
his black silhouette bending to and fro in
the failing light.

" The man turned away, and walked
towards the bed, but the woman did not
look round, nor even seem to be aware
of his presence.   He stood in uncertainty
for a minute, looking down on her, and
then he said, ' You'd better go to the
workhouse.'

" But she took no notice.

" ' You'd better go ? ' he said.   ' You'll
be all right there,' and he stooped down
and put a shilling in the withered hand
that touched the bare floor by his feet.
Then he walked to the window again,
picked up the chisel, and left the room.
The wooden staircase creaked under his
weight, and his echoing steps came fainter
and fainter from below.

" The woman lay on the floor, the sun set and the river hurried by. The wind rushed in through the broken window, bringing the damp of the rising mists, and of the marshy fields. Night fell and the woman lay there still. Through the darkness she moaned, 'Give me time, give me a little time!' The wind beat down the mists, and the stars smiled on the earth beneath. A spear of light shot through the window; it crossed the floor but left in darkness the corner where she tossed. The river rushed on, black and swollen, and the osiers bent and swayed in the starlight. The dawn broke slowly in the east, and the blackness of the wintry morn changed to grey. Across the sky stole the rain-clouds, huge and shapeless in the niggard light. The wind blew fresh from the river—the tide had turned, and was flowing quietly inland; the breeze played with the woman's hair, it lifted a grey lock in

sport, and then fled lest she should wake.
The shadows faded as the cold light
broke over the floor ; it stole over the
hearth, it penetrated to the dark corner,
and creeping down the bare walls it
reached the yellow face of the dead."

He ceased, and no one spoke.

A man passed by on the opposite side,
and they watched his shadow lingering
from lamp to lamp, as though unwilling
to follow its master.

The silence grew oppressive. Brinton
was still leaning on the parapet, with his
face turned away from the others, and
his eyes fixed on the river below.

"I wonder what became of the man
who went back and put the shilling into
her hand," said Nina, at last.

"He is alive," said Brinton, in a voice
that made everybody shudder.

"Are you the man ?" cried Lofthouse,
the first to find his voice.

"Ah, no," said Brinton, quietly,
"Alas, I was the other man."

They started, but he kept his face turned away. Nobody spoke. All felt that sympathy was useless, and the words died on their lips.

He misunderstood their silence, and all would have given anything in the world at that moment to have explained it.

He turned his face, and began to walk slowly away.

" Come back," Nina tried to say, but the words stuck in her throat.

They listened to his footsteps in the distance, they strained their eyes to see his retreating figure, but in a few moments the echoes had died away, and he was lost in the night, swallowed up in the shadows of the great city.

" I cannot bear it," said Nina. " I will go after him, and speak to him. Let me go by myself." And she hurried away in the direction Brinton had taken.

The others sat in silence for a long time, each absorbed in his own thoughts, each haunted by the voice of the man whom they were never to see again.

By and by Nina returned, and sat down without saying a word.

Nobody asked her if she had found him. They saw it in her eyes, and they mastered their curiosity, and asked no questions.

Thus they sat watching the river, till their thoughts were broken by the noise that a long string of market carts made in passing slowly over the bridge.

Suddenly a flush ran through the sky.

" It is the dawn," said Lofthouse.

" The dawn!" said McWhirter, rubbing his eyes. He had fallen into a quiet doze with his head on the parapet, and on awaking, was, with the logic of his race, connecting the approach of morning with the approach of breakfast. "Eh, mon!" said he, "but that's a gran' sicht for a sharp-set chiel !"

As he spoke the air was filled with light, and everything took a clear and sharp outline. The hulls of the barges stood out boldly from the grey water, the deserted quays separated themselves from the bulwark of boats, the lamps grew fainter and fainter.

A bird began to call from somewhere up the river. Eastwards over the sleeping city stretched a broad belt of smoke-coloured cloud, frayed at the edges with gold, and pierced with tawny fissures which were widening slowly. Above the belt floated a rosy cloud ; they watched it for a long time growing brighter and brighter, and the light rushing towards the west. It was day.

On the incoming tide moved three barges with little brown sails spread to catch what wind there was from the

south.   They stretched lazily across the
stream, narrowly missing one another,
and then tacked and passed under the
bridge, the men tugging at the clumsy
oars, which gave forth a monotonous
" creak," " creak," at every pull.

From the last of the barges, *The
Sprightly Polly*, painted pea-green with
a white stripe, curled a blue smoke, and
from the cabin there came the clatter of
cups, and the sound of a woman's voice.

"They are wiser than we," said
Patrick. "Only hear how the kettle
sings! I swear I can smell the rashers
frizzling. Let us go and hunt for our
breakfast."

A coffee-stall on the Surrey side gave
them a warm welcome. The keen
morning air had given all a prodigious
appetite. Nina seized a slice of thick
bread-and-butter, Patrick a hunch of
cake, Lofthouse a piece of bread and
marmalade, and Martell a jam-tart.

"I always love a London egg," said McWhirter, peeling one that was hard-boiled; "they are sae wholesome!"

"Morning, Jack," said a workman, glancing curiously at Nina. "How are you?"

"Not what you'd call grand," returned the coffee-stall keeper. I've got a cold in my head."

"Cold! Why that's nothing. I've had one for twenty years, off and on, you know. That's a fine young man you've got there; is he married?" said the workman, winking in the direction of Patrick.

"No. He's a widower," replied Jack, entering into the joke.

"Ah; I suppose he married for money before, but now he'll marry for looks," said the other.

But these personalities were too much for Nina. The scalding coffee had made the colour come back into her

7*

cheeks, she told herself; but she knew
the others would search for a more
ridiculous reason.

"Mr. McWhirter, a hansom, please!"
she said, hastily; and indeed it was
time, for the early workmen who had
left their women-folk asleep, were troop-
ing over the bridge, and beginning to
take too lively an interest in the sleepy
members of the Paradox Club.

"Quickly!" she entreated, when the
cab rattled up with McWhirter. "I
don't regret it," she said to herself,
as though defiantly protesting against
the faint voice which whispered that
she was foolish to have yielded to
Patrick's taunt; and that this escapade
was going a little too far, even for Nina
Lindon.

Then catching sight of her white and
tear-stained face in the glass at her
elbow she sighed, "But I never will
again, never! How hideous I look! I

wonder what he could have thought of me!"

And when she was not musing over what Brinton had told her of his history, she was wondering what Patrick could have thought, all the way to Kensington.

ON BEING ANTICIPATED.

V.

ON BEING ANTICIPATED.

NEARLY four months had passed, and the lovers had seen but little of one another. In July, Nina, to Patrick's despair, went abroad, and did not return till the end of September. It was remarked at the office that Patrick's temper had changed for the worse, and that he took an unnatural interest in the foreign mail. Through the stifling heat of August he sat at his desk, apparently absorbed in the secrets of a ledger, but the pile of papers at his hand did not diminish, whereas the floor was strewn with the fragments of unfinished letters.

Business notes 'that he had formerly succeeded in answering in a week now took a fortnight, and he displayed a command of sarcasm that astonished his fellow clerks, and dismayed the head of his department, who—too suspicious a man ever to have fallen in love—began to predict embezzlement, and long for the *dénoûment*.

Occasionally Patrick tried verse-making, but his results convinced him he was wrong to laugh at Lofthouse. He cursed the mixture of weakness and courage that had led him to despatch one little poem to Nina, and an hour after post-time he would have cheerfully paid a month's salary—in anticipation— to have had the letter in his hands again.

When the lovers met at last, Patrick instantly detected the shyness that absence had bred in Nina, and of course put it down to coldness. Nina, on her part, finding him a little distant in his manner, tried hard to pretend to herself that he no longer cared for her, but the song of happiness that grew louder day by day in her heart, convicted her head of charming insincerity.

One November afternoon Nina and Miss Ward arrived early by appointment at the Paradox Club, and settled down before the fire to a good talk.

"We have not been seeing so much of Mr. Weld lately," said Miss Ward, "and I for one am not sorry. I'm sure you don't mind my saying so, dear Nina, but I think him a most objectionable youth. You know I always thought, dear," she continued, "that it was most imprudent of you to go about with him as you did, most imprudent! Think if anybody had got to hear of it!"

"I'll tell him," said Nina, "and you mustn't mind him laughing at you, Charlotte! Why, we have known each other ever since we were that high."

"Of course, dear, I don't suppose he'll eat you," said Charlotte. "Indeed, I always thought him a very mild youth, and oh, so plain!"

The odious imputation that Patrick was not only a tame cat, but an ugly one, galled Nina nearly as much as her friend had intended. Patrick plain! She could hardly refrain from calling attention on the spot to the dimple in his chin.

"He's not so intellectual looking as Mr. Chapple," she said, "but you know, Charlotte, you always had a partiality for men with bald heads and knobby foreheads. Now, I *hate* a knobby forehead!"

"Ah, Mr. Chapple has indeed the expression of a thinker!" sighed Miss Ward, sentimentally.

"What a marked interest he takes in you, Charlotte," said Nina, who could not forgive her friend for saying that Patrick was "mild" when she knew perfectly well that he was nothing of the sort.

"My dear Nina, what an idea!" said Miss Ward, much fluttered at anybody's giving shape to the thought which had possessed her for months. "What could have put such an idea into your head?"

"Of course I guessed it," said Nina, maliciously. "Why how could I help it, unless I had kept my eyes shut?"

"My dear Nina," began the lady, intensely delighted, "I——"

"Anybody can see you understand each other perfectly, Charlotte," said Nina. "I am surprised he has not spoken to you. Why here he comes!" she broke off, as Chapple entered the room, and advanced towards them.

As the reader knows, Chapple had already proposed to Nina a few months before, and Nina was well aware that he did not care in the least for Miss Ward, though his sentimental attitude towards every woman he came across favoured the idea that he was ready to make a fool of himself at the slightest provocation. In reality Nina felt she had acted meanly towards her friend and Chapple in hinting at a match between them ; but, quick as most women are to believe what she wished to believe, she decided that by a little dexterity Chapple's affections might be transferred to Charlotte, giving herself peace, and her friend happiness.

Besides, had not Charlotte just called Patrick a most objectionable youth ?

Now Chapple had come thus early to the Club in the hope of seeing Nina alone, and pressing his suit once more. The kind and gentle way in which she had rejected him, so as not to wound his feelings, had whispered to his conceit that she must in the long run yield to his fascinations ; and he quickly seized his opportunity when McWhirter was engaging Miss Ward in conversation.

But Nina was obdurate.

" Is there no hope ? " he pleaded.

" None, Mr. Chapple," she answered, with great firmness.

" I would wait years," he replied, sadly. " Years, Miss Lindon ! If you would only give me a little hope, I would wait five years."

Nina gave a start. " Five years," thought she. " What an absurd thing to say ! I shall be quite old then."

" Five years did I say ! " echoed Chapple, who had mistaken her movement, and thought he had been too precipitate. " Nay, I would wait ten, willingly, Miss Lindon."

" Good heavens ! what devotion ! " thought Nina. " What shall I be like in ten years ? "

To put an end to the scene, and to save him pain once for all, she replied :

"There is no use in waiting, Mr. Chapple, not the faintest.   I do not love you."

[1] "We stand at a turning-point in our lives, a crisis," he said, solemnly, determined to make a last effort.   "Oh, Miss Lindon, do not let us make a mistake! I stand awed and reverent before the mysteries of your heart ; but let not my inexperienced tongue put my future in jeopardy."

When he understood that his inexperienced tongue did put him in some jeopardy, he reluctantly subsided, promising himself, however, that he would sound Miss Ward later on as to Nina's true feelings.   His vanity would not yet allow him to admit that he had no chance.

"Here comes Mr. Lofthouse!" cried

[1] The author desires to express his indebtedness to the authoress of "Margaret Dunmore; or The Unitary Home,"

Miss Ward, suddenly. "Now we are going to hear all about the books we ought to read. We really *must* belong to Mudie's, Nina dear, mustn't we ? Oh ! how I wish that somebody would lend me a pencil."

And while McWhirter was deliberating with his usual caution whether he would cut his pencil before offering it to her, or wait till she had returned it, and then cut it, Lofthouse began as follows :

"As one on whom Literature has left some mark, and as one who would fain leave some mark on Literature, I compare myself to a traveller standing where many ways meet. The path of Tragedy is too steep for me to climb, and many falls await him who would descend to the smiling valley of Comedy. Nor will I face the nettles which choke the stony road of Criticism, nor the dust of the highway of Theology, nor the mists of

Philosophy, nor the mazes of History. But more by choice than necessity I turn to the winding lane of Poetry, fenced with blackberries and hazels, with here and there a cluster of honeysuckle well out of reach. A gap reveals the corn-fields, golden brown once; but now only the white of the stubble shows. The harvest is over, and the mighty reapers, the great poets, have left me only the gleanings of the hedges hung with the wheat that the brambles pulled from the cart, as it went slowly up to the granary. They have left me only a few half-hidden flowers which fade at my touch. I press eagerly on, but everywhere find myself anticipated, everywhere the barren earth strikes my eye, till I come to where a few tiny blades of green are pushing through the clods, showing that there will be a harvest for those who come after me.

"But what have my contemporaries been

doing meanwhile ? Some have sung so sweetly that those who have listened to their melodies, have fancied they saw before them the ripe ears bending in the wind, and the youths and maidens of the Golden Age driving their sheep homeward in the setting sun. Others have sung of olden times with such fire that the bystanders have turned their eyes backwards, thinking they heard the clash of steel and the thunder of chariot wheels. One has wandered to the shore, and his verses echo back to us the triumph of the sea, and the confusion of its victory. Others have sailed to foreign lands and have brought back rare and beautiful flowers, and strange seeds, but seeds that always run wild, and flowers that always wither in English soil. Though many poets have nourished and cherished these exotics, useless is their labour, and wasted their time, for the product is but a weed after all.

8

"But though the harvest be already gathered, and the people contented with the bread therefrom, still there remains to all the poets the sky for beauty, and the earth for truth, and the wind for melody, and though they cannot rival the work of the reapers who single-handed cut the ripe corn, their words should cause fresh seed to be sown for future generations to gather fresh harvests.

"But leaving metaphor for a while, I assert that mine is the most miserable lot of any author ; for I am continually being anticipated by the great wits of the day. Do I plan some scathing verses on turn-coats, and Mr. Swinburne is announced to have a poem breathing fire and slaughter on that subject in the press. I can assure my hearers that the rough draft of ' Dr. Jekyl and Mr. Hyde' was in my desk (of course the names in my version were different, and Mr. Hyde was eventually converted and saved by

the Salvation Army), when to my utter
confusion I picked up Mr. Stevenson's
work on the counter of a well-known
Holborn bookseller. So much was in-
volved in the issue that I felt it was only
my duty to the Public to demand an ex-
planation from Mr. Stevenson. But the
answer was not satisfactory. I am indeed continually being anticipated! A
certain study of Shelley stopped the
publication of a burlesque of his character I had undertaken as a *jeu d'esprit*:
a certain translation of Æschylus showed
me how ridiculous it was for more than
one poet to set about turning Bohn's
Classical Library into verse. After
finishing a volume of ' Confessions of a
Realist,' it struck me that to be natural-
istic one ought properly to lose one's
character, which is hardly original; after
reading a Scotch tale, I saw in a flash
what an important place slow summer
sunsets may fill in a three-volume novel.

" But the fate of being anticipated has saved me from the vice of being popular. There are so many dubious byways that lead to semi-success in Literature that I am thankful I have returned to the crossroads. I might have written tragedies, and, purchasing one hundred copies myself, and sending one hundred for review, have had a second edition called for 'in less than three months.' As I have a decent ear for other people's metres my volume of verse might have elicited an essay of four columns and a half in some literary journal on the paucity of double rhymes in English. But to keep oneself constantly before the public needs a genius for advertising as well as considerable agility; and it is a ticklish thing to play battledore and shuttlecock with one's friends on Parnassus. Though a clever lady novelist has shown us how profitable it is to expose one's sex and how easy it is to expose oneself, I leave the field of fiction to the rival schools that are acquainted with the scenery of Central Africa, and skilled in the dissection of a housemaid's heart.

" Turning to criticism I would say that authors are extremely inconsiderate to their reviewers. They forget that a critic has generally to master in two days what it takes an author years to study.

" A considerate author will therefore append to his preface a list of the authorities he has consulted. Such thoughtfulness is not thrown away. For without it how could a reviewer be omniscient on every subject, from the structure of the sonnet to a treatise on Civil Law and the State? Specialists as critics are out of date. Such an outcry has been raised about biassed critics, that obviously the only course for an editor is to hand the book to a man who knows nothing at all about the subject. And indeed there is no reason why London should not follow the example of the provincial press. But it is injudicious for literary men to clamour much about unfair reviewing, for it is rarely good policy to disparage a paper you are dying to contribute to. Log-rolling also has been made too much of. Few critics find it practicable to keep a literary friendship alive; the public are so fond of a good rousing attack. The race of reviewers is indeed much maligned! Which critic shall we pity most, him who knows more than his author, or him who knows less? While the one is annoyed by the mistakes he finds on every page, the other is irritated at finding none. Perhaps the censor of Poetry is the luckiest, and the censor of Theology the unluckiest; while nothing is so exasperating as other people's dogmas, nothing is sweeter than the reflection that the repulsion you feel at the sight of a fresh volume of songs is balanced by the attraction your critique invariably has for the songster.

"Who envies now either author or critic? Happier is the honest book-maker, or the weary editor. And Publishers? Their motto should be 'Great wit to madness nearly is allied;' for their doors are crowded with *littérateurs* who to demonstrate that they are possessed of genius produce works which prove insanity runs in the family. A Publisher indeed is assailed by so many poets, receives so many novels, devises so many schemes for the decent interment of still-born literary infants, that he would soon give up the ghost were it not for the Review Book, a tonic of great strength and bitterness. Some authors however affirm that the book that interests him the most is his Cheque Book."

"What is the pleasantest thing you know, Weld?" asked Lofthouse, disregarding Martell's audible aside that though a woman's vanity always saves her from egotism, a Poet's egotism never saves him from vanity.

"To box with a man three stone lighter than myself," answered Patrick; "or to swim in a sea rough enough to make one's friends needlessly alarmed."

Nina drew mentally a picture of his brown head among the waves, and smiled to herself with pleasure. She, like Isopel Berners, loved the sun and wind.

"What is yours, Charlotte?" she asked.

"To exchange confidences with a friend," said Miss Ward.

"And the pleasantest thing you know, Mr. McWhirter?"

"If you had asked me the nicest thing I ken, I should ha' replied the leetarary circle of Peebles. But as you——"

"Mine," interrupted Chapple, "is a man who can talk sense."

"And mine," said the Poet, "is a woman who can talk nonsense."

"Yours is propaganda, I suppose?" said Patrick, turning to the Socialist.

" Not at all," answered Martell; " mine is a Society journal. I love Satire, and these papers are living satires on the age. They disgust you, I suppose ? "

" I loathe a dust-bin," returned the Irishman.

" You are disgusted with these papers, and you read them!" exclaimed Martell.

Patrick did not know what to answer.

" The Society papers," he said, after a pause, " are scavengers' carts into which everything unclean is thrown. Useful they certainly are; but they taint the air through which they pass."

" I prefer the men who collect the mud to the men who throw it," said the Socialist. " Why do you condemn those who, after all, give you what you like to read ? "

" One loathes it *because* it has a faint fascination for one," cried Nina, coming to the rescue.

8*

"We hate scandal," said everybody in a breath.

"The reason why a man hates scandal is that, when he .hears other people's failings being discussed, he knows that his turn may come next," said Martell. "Scandal is the salt that keeps Society from putrefying. If our friends did not pry into all our affairs, and if we were sure of not being found out, what records we should all have ! What passions should we not gratify if our friends were as obtuse as our enemies !"

" These papers make us take such an unhealthy and low view of mankind," began Lofthouse.

"Since we know in our hearts how much weaker and meaner, and more dishonest we are than our friends think us," replied Martell, "we may be pretty sure that they are much baser than we think them."

" It is impossible to form real friendships with such views in one's brain," interposed Lofthouse, again.

"Friendship! Utopia!" cried the Socialist. "Why should we be afraid of whispering what we think is the truth about our friends, for if guilty they deserve to be exposed and punished, and if innocent, what good can their friendship do us, when such suspicion can come between ?"

"Are these your own or Zola's principles ?" asked the Poet.

"Mine," replied Martell, "Zola is quite optimistic at times. But Zola does certainly generally destroy illusion. He tears to shreds the pernicious glamour which surrounds so many poets. I am told that the favourite reading of educated girls of nineteen or twenty is the sickly sentiment of Swinburne—

"'The lilies and languors of virtue ;
The roses and raptures of vice.'

Now I say that it is impossible for any

woman who has studied Zola to be injured by Swinburne."

"What *woman* could possibly read Zola!" exclaimed the Poet, in a rage.

"What girl could admire Swinburne!" groaned Chapple.

"Good Heavens, I have read both!" whispered Nina to Patrick.

"I suppose you admire 'A Mummer's Wife, Martell?" asked Lofthouse.

"Oh I don't defend Moore," continued the Socialist, "though he has drawn several good portraits. Dick's, for instance, cannot be surpassed. But generally he mixes vulgarity with indelicacy, and he is often coarse without being clever. Now how different is his method from Sterne's!"

"Sterne who first taught the English to refine coarseness, and enjoy indelicacy!" said Lofthouse.

"Just so. True views of Literature are rapidly gaining ground. Psychological truth and fidelity to detail are now given their right place, and Daudet, Maupassant, and the rest are treading in the footsteps of Swift and Balzac."

"Maupassant disgusts me," said Nina.

"That is because your point of view is not the scientific one."

"And pray," burst out Lofthouse, who had been simmering with indignation, "what is your scientific point of view, and what, after all, is this great realistic school of Literature? Its masters condemn it; its pupils condemn it; its results condemn it. Its whole beginning and end is one long condemnation. The difference between the antagonistic schools is simply one of health. When people are diseased in mind or body, or crossed in love, or afflicted with black bile they naturally exclaim, 'How truthful is Balzac, how realistic is Zola, how faithful is Swift!' When people are pure in mind and body they delight in Borrow and Jefferies, Wordsworth, or Whitman if you will."

"A most misleading distinction!" said Martell.

"Balzac who kept himself up till four o'clock every morning with black coffee, and Swift who was diseased, naturally had a contempt for men who spent their days in the woods and fields and bathed in the open sea. The man who gets up when the sun sets always despises him who gets up when it rises."

"The Idealists can never bear dissection, whether it be of a rabbit or human nature," rejoined Martell.

"The Realists dissect their fellows through the microscope of self," said Lofthouse. "Zola's books are photographs it is true, but photographs of himself. I object to have that eternal face of his peeping from each fresh costume."

" Nonsense, my dear fellow," said Martell. " It's very evident that you only know Balzac and Zola from hearsay. Everybody who hasn't your simple tastes isn't therefore diseased. Milk and honey was all very well for the Golden Age, but it palls on the Nineteenth Century."

" But seriously," returned Lofthouse, " what is this cloud that all the Realists are under ? "

" It is the cloud of existence," said the Socialist. " In youth it perplexes us, in manhood it threatens us, in old age it crushes us. Disillusion underlies everything. Science has shown that individual man has no more to do with his character than with his coming into the world. For the majority life has more pain than pleasure."

" Nonsense," cried Patrick and Lofthouse, in a breath.

" ' A little sweet doth kill much bitterness,'" thought Nina, as she glanced at Patrick.

"'Where the wicked cease from troubling, and the weary are at rest,'" quoted Miss Ward.

"His stomach is a bit wrang," said McWhirter to Chapple.

"I fear, Mr. McWhirter, we must seek for a deeper and more mysterious concatenation of circumstances."

"Even supposing you are right, and the majority experience more pleasure than pain, we Socialists object to the cruelty of the minority writhing, while the rest look on and laugh. We realize that we do not know why we are here, and that we are merely puppets in Nature's hands. It is not so much that we object to our own suffering, as we object to being the instruments for torturing our fellows. We are continually, consciously or unconsciously, harming others. Thus women often die in childbirth; and there are hundreds of parallel cases."

"It certainly is very cruel," said Lofthouse, thoughtfully, "when somebody falls in love with you, and you cannot reciprocate."

"Most terrible, most terrible," sighed Chapple. "It makes one feel so much to blame."

"Oh, in love there is not much cruelty," remarked Martell. "He who desires and cannot have, is at least spared having and not desiring. But to return to my argument. I believe that out of every hundred people, eighty wish in their hearts that they had never been born."

"Only conform to Nature and you will be content," said Lofthouse. "You say that your creed teaches that life is an evil. Why not adopt another which finds in Childhood Innocence, in Youth Power, in Old Age Content? When you see the barren fields of your school,

and our fruitful meadows, don't you suspect that there must be a serious flaw in
your system of tillage? It seems to me
that where the Idealists reap Happiness,
the Naturalists gather Unhappiness.
Adopt our plan, and surely the end will
justify the means."

" We might be dupes," said the Socialist ; " but the age of Disenchantment has
set in. But do not turn away with the
idea that we find no pleasure in Life, for
we cannot help ourselves. The world is
indeed a stage, and all the actors, enjoy
tasting or touching or seeing. But
whereas you, Lofthouse, fancy that you
eat and drink and love by choice, we see
that you are forced to do what you do,
say what you say, and play the part you
are cast for."

"Well, then, play your part and be
happy."

" Our knowledge takes away much of
our interest in life."

" But you must have some compensation."

" Well," replied Martell, " we are profoundly interested in ourselves."

" There is one thing you have totally overlooked," replied Lofthouse, " and that is doing good. You blame Nature for everything, blame yourself for much. It is man who torments man, robs, cheats, and murders him, and then sits down and sheds crocodile tears. If all strove to do good, the world would be happy to-morrow."

" You beg the question altogether ! " exclaimed Martell. " I tell you we are Determinists. What on earth is the use of telling the murderer whose parents were vicious to be good ! His brain is as diseased as the drunkard's body."

" But do you ever try ? " persisted the Poet. " You never do. As Jefferies says, if you sit down and argue you can't walk to a place, you can't walk there, but if you start off you will arrive all right."

Everybody laughed at his lack of logic.

"It is you Fatalists who are under delusion," he explained. "When a man makes a fool of himself in public, do you mean to say that he really believes he couldn't have helped it?"

"What do you think, Chapple?" said Martell.

"I fear that too often the unhappy individual deserves severe reprehension," replied Chapple.

"There you are!" cried Lofthouse. "You see the evidence is on my side. Well, the long and the short of it is, Martell, that when you sit down to breakfast you contend that you must eat salmon and not herrings, whereas I contend you need not appropriate all the marmalade."

"Well, if you like to put it that way,

I don't mind.   The present and future are contained in the past."

"So that is Determinism in a nut-shell," concluded the Poet.   "You Fatal-ists are simply men who are muddled at the bare idea of an alternative."

"We shall very soon get muddled if we keep on going round in a circle," said Martell.   "We had better drop the subject."

"Before we do," replied the Poet, "let me quote one of the most beauti-ful truths ever written: I mean that of Borrow : ' Life is sweet, brother. There's night and day, brother, both sweet things; sun, moon, and stars, brother, all sweet things ; there's like-wise a wind on the heath.   Life is very sweet, brother.' "

"I was talking of the poor," persisted Martell.   "How many of them have the wind on the heath ?   When you are working sixteen hours a day you don't see much sun, and you are too tired ever to notice the moon and the stars."

Lofthouse saw that he could make no impression, and he looked towards Patrick for aid. Very soon the three were quarrelling about Ireland.

"Union *versus* Home Rule is the struggle of Sense with Sentiment," said Martell. "Our aim should be to unite the two, in which lies the secret of successful government."

"English doctors will never cure Ireland," said Patrick, "by persisting in their useless steel pills, and iron for tonics."

"Better than the homœopathy of Home Rule, and such like quackery," said Martell. "The arrows of the Parnellites fly very wide of the mark."

"But the boomerang of Coercion recoils on the user," rejoined Patrick, hotly.

Miss Ward had paid very little atten-

tion to either the paper or the conversation that evening, for Nina's words
about Chapple's marked attentions to her
came back again and again. Every
little courtesy that he paid her that evening, the way in which he agreed with
everything she said, the sympathetic
looks he threw at her from time to time,
all confirmed the suspicion she had
harboured so long of his being in love
with her. While Lofthouse and Martell
were still debating on Determinism, he
rose and gently drew her aside. His
manner was mysterious, his words still
more so. To her agitated mind every
sentence showed that *une certaine tension*
existed between them.

"Miss Ward," he at last said, solemnly,
"I have something to say that I trust
will please you. I have long loved——"

"Oh, Mr. Chapple!" replied the lady,
with modest confusion. "This is so un-
expected, so unlooked for."

" Then you know ? " asked Chapple, surprised ; "you know how dear——"

" Hush ! " she broke in. " Speak lower, please, or some one will hear."

" Miss Ward," said he, earnestly, sinking his voice to a whisper, " I have long loved——"

" Long ? " said she, softly. " Then dear Nina——" She stopped herself from adding, " was right."

"She told me there was no hope for me," said Chapple, a trifle sadly.

" No hope ! " said the lady, indignant at such feminine double-facedness. " No hope ! Why, over and over again she assured me——"

" Dear Miss Ward," interrupted Chapple. " Thank you so much, so very much. My heart is now at rest. But a simple, innocent girl may have depths that a man can never fathom ! I thought all along it would be better to speak straight out to you, but at first

I was afraid of being repulsed. 'I will speak to her dearest friend,' I said to myself."

"I thought once she was my friend," said Miss Ward, surprised at Chapple still pursuing the subject; "but after what you say, I will never speak to her again!"

"Come," said Chapple, astonished at the warmth he thought she was displaying on his behalf. "Nina was naturally modest. Dear girl! she did not like to avow it at first, she who has lived wholly in sensations and emotions."

"Modest!" cried the lady, thoroughly aroused. "Modest!" I call such modesty false modesty. Why, she told me this evening that nothing could have pleased her more."

"It does seem a little odd," he mused, "when she said so decidedly just now that it could never be a question of love between us."

9

" It's really too bad," said Miss Ward, extremely angry at the base way in which she thought Chapple had been kept from proposing to her.

" Ah, but *now* we understand each other," he pursued, leaning forward confidentially, and bringing his head nearer.

To his surprise, he found Miss Ward's head on his shoulder. " What an extraordinary girl! Is she ill?" he said to himself, growing alarmed. " Shall I bring you a glass of water?" he added, kindly. " Perhaps it is the heat that has overcome you!"

" Oh, no, no," murmured she, with her eyes shut. " How easily they might have parted us!"

A cold shudder ran through Chapple's frame. Could she think he was in love with *her?* Impossible!

" Miss Ward," he said, stiffly, " I must beg you, I really must, to remember that——"

One glance at his face showed the lady the unspeakable error she had committed.

But a step and a voice close behind them changed the hatred in their hearts to a feeling of self-preservation. " Not a word ! " they had barely time to whisper to one another before Nina stood before them.

"Will you not come and play to us, Charlotte ?" she said, in a matter-of-fact voice that made the victims writhe.

"A Little Summer Shower" was given, to the delight of the audience. Chapple, while listening to the music, had recovered his equanimity. A desire to be magnanimous stole into his breast. After all, he reflected, she is not the first who has fallen in love with me. Nor indeed the last, he added, for he began to feel sure that Nina, too, had a flame for him. The music stopped, and he hastened to Miss Ward's side to show that he bore her no ill-feeling.

"It recalls Nature so admirably," he said. "One actually hears the patter of the raindrops on the leaves, the songs of the birds, and the wind, sad presage of autumn, as it sighs round the trees. Then comes a lull, and lifting one's head to the sunshine, one is delighted to find the 'Little Summer Shower' is over."

A little shock of admiration ran through the company that he should have expressed so boldly the mind of all. But Chapple settled his spectacles firmly, and continued, unconscious of the surprise he had created. "After hearing such a gem of modern thought and musical setting, one is tempted to risk a disappointment in other branches of the Arts. Mr. Lofthouse, what, may I ask, are your views on Art?"

"Art for Art's sake!" said Lofthouse. "Art is my mistress."

"His mistress could do very well

without a good many of her lovers,"
whispered Martell, aside.

"When I was young"—he was twenty-
two—"and foolish," continued the Poet,
" I joined a Society whose object was to
raise both classes and masses to its own
level. Our main theory was that what-
ever you want done in Art you should
do yourself. Thus the artist who designs
a mantelpiece should cast it himself, so
that the work may have ' feeling.' It is
better, we said, that the shovel should be a
failure than that it should be mechanical,
and lack individuality. One of us made
a design and engraved it himself on
wood for *The Soul String.* It was certainly full of feeling. I never saw anything like it before or since. It was a
triumph of individuality. But the subject
—a tea-kettle, in black and white, with
the lid off—pleased the critics even less
than the execution. (This was of course
a great triumph.) And not one of them
saw the allegory ! "

"But the masses still decorate their sprigged wall-paper with chromos from Landseer," said Martell.

"We started an upholsterer's shop," explained the Poet, "but we found the people were too enthusiastically degraded. Some friends who bought the Pisan chairs said they didn't mind the high price, but they must have comfort; while others declared that they couldn't understand why a chair that had three legs should be twice as dear as one that had four! But at last we died. You see we were heavily handicapped by the fact of several of our members having had all the disadvantages of a university education."

"Can you not repeat," said Chapple, persistently, "some of your efforts in Art, so that I may have an idea of your school?"

"I remember one poem," said Lofthouse, "but I must tell you it will give

you no idea of our productions, because——"

"It is far better," said Martell.

But Lofthouse paid no heed to the
taunt, and began:

"*The fire burns bright : the amber flickering
       tongues
   Chase through the room, and on thy fair
       white throat
     The slanting shadows wake.
   Ah! I could watch each breath that thou dost
       take,
   Till, through the low-banked clouds the red
       morn break,
   Far must I be by dawn, far hence by day,
       'Tis the last night!*

"*The fire burns low: the smothered embers
       faint,
   Glimmer on rusty ash, and powdery flake,
     That fell so quietly.
   Ah! I could list thy voice till faded be
   The sorrowing dusk which now enfoldeth
       thee.
   Far must I be by dawn, far hence by day,
       'Tis the last night!*"

Patrick and Nina passed into the quiet street, and began to walk homeward. They talked of the most trivial things, but each remark carried a secret and a sweeter meaning. Each sentence twisted itself into something different, each word that was lost to the head found an echo in the heart. "Does she love me?" said Patrick, a thousand times to himself. "Does he love me still?" wondered Nina.

Never had she seemed so charming to him as on that night. Her soft voice, her profile in shadow, the rustle of her dress, all revealing how much was hidden, how much lay beneath her tantalizing indifference, were as the waving curtain, past which steal light and music. Yet at a single word from him the picture might fade away, as it had done before. The love that he fancied he read in her eyes might be but the reflection from his own, and to

stretch forth his hand might be to destroy the illusion he had created. Did
she love him? Her voice said Yes, his
experience, No. He knew the lines:

> "When maidens innocently young
>   Say aften what they never mean,
> Ne'er mind their pretty, lying tongue
>   But tent the language o' their een."

And he was sure they applied to every
one except her.

Meanwhile Nina was puzzling over
what her heart had told her a thousand
times. Why was he so odd to-night?
Why did he change so quickly when
he must know that she only appeared
cold to avoid helpless embarrassment?
Why was everything so vague and
shadowy when, when——? Why did
he keep on talking of the same thing?
He did not really care for her, he was
merely amusing himself; and now she
remembered that when she had been

abroad he had not written to her for a whole week.

"You don't forget," said he, "that you said you wanted to see the Mile-End Road on a Saturday night?"

"No, I want to go, for I am beginning to take your view of London; and, after all, why should we not be content where we are?"

The word "content" jarred on Patrick. He wished to see Nina as discontented as himself.

"I am sick of London," he said, with considerable energy. "I don't mind where I go, so long as I get out of it. Then I should feel less restless."

"Why would you feel less restless?" said Nina.

Directly afterwards she blushed that she should have asked, but she strained her ears for the answer.

"Ah, you know why, Nina?" he said.

Her heart beat fast as she tried to answer carelessly :

" Patrick, are we not friends ? "

" I want love," he said.

He braced himself for the disillusionment. He fancied it must come, and perhaps in the effort to meet it his voice had grown hard.

Why was he so cold, she said to herself. The avowal had come at last, but oh, so differently to what she had expected. He must have seen all along how much she loved him, and now he spoke in a voice as though of an everyday thing. But he loved her. What could she answer ? How could she tell him when he made it so difficult ?

" I think you are a little ungrateful."

She did not know whether she was reproaching him for not having broken the silence on the subject before, or for having broken it at all.

But Patrick could not see into the

subtleties of a woman's heart, subtleties
that a woman raises in mere self-defence
against disappointment, subtleties that
are swept away at the first touch of
love. The words were spoken, and he
repeated them mechanically to himself
without looking for any meaning behind
them. He realized that there was no
hope, and that was all.

"Ungrateful!" he repeated, bitterly;
"Well, yes, perhaps I am ungrateful,
when I have your friendship."

He said no more, and they walked
on in silence. Nina's heart sank at
every step. What did it all mean, she
asked herself piteously? Why had this
cruel thing happened? It was like
awakening in the cold night after a
dream of sunshine. She did not realize
how many times the things she had
said in jest he had taken in earnest.
She had taught him to dread her wit,
and this was the result.

At length they reached her home, and they separated.

Nina sat alone, long after he had left her. He must come back, she thought ; he must come back. He cannot leave me without a word. He must come back.

Patrick strode homewards in tragic wrath. He damned the whole affair. He consigned the whole sex to oblivion, with the exception of Nina. "Of course, I knew she didn't love me," he said, bitterly. "Why did I persist? Hasn't she told me, or as good as told me, twice before it's of not the slightest use? It's the same as at Porlock. Friends! Curse that word—friendship! Why was her voice so soft? Oh, but she says she is fond of me. She is in love with some one else !"

And while he was seeking to excuse Nina's behaviour, she was reading over the letters he had addressed to the

Continent ; and now, for the first time, the passages of studied indifference that he had carefully inserted through the remote fear of being laughed at, struck her in their untrue light.

THE MILE-END ROAD.

VI.

THE MILE-END ROAD.

THE last Saturday night in November saw the Mile-End Road white with snow. Snow lay thick on the booths that had been rigged up for the market night; on the tarpaulins of the hay waggons that were moving slowly towards Stratford, the carters plodding, with downcast eyes, at their horses' heads; on the red lamps and gilded balcony of " The Blind Beggar," the inn that defies its near rivals " The Vine Tavern " and " The White Hart."

Light, the fierce light of paraffin, flared through the darkness from hun-

dreds of stalls, and fell on a broad
sheet of snow, through which a black
river (the track worn by the horses'
hoofs) wound its narrow way. Light,
quivering light, fell everywhere. The
paraffin burst in orange flames from
the sugar-loaf tin lamps of the booths,
or spent itself in streamers of blue
fire, hissing when the wind caught it.
Light darted in wavering strips over
the broad roadway to the dark side
beyond, falling suddenly on the face
of the countryman and his three white
horses, who had just emerged from the
gloom. It danced over the roped heads
of the horses, and gleamed on the straw-
plait which tied their tails in a hard knot,
showing that they were for sale; and
then it fell elsewhere, leaving the
countryman and his beasts but indistinct figures.

On the broad white footpath, beaten
hard by thousands of feet, a torrent of

people was pouring eastwards, past
the ballad-singer who, standing on a
rough platform of boards, with flaming
jet dropping liquid fire to the ground
below, sang his verses to a ring of
boys whose shadows lengthened and
shot out over the snow; past the
baskets of rusty iron, over which bent
old women whose shadows mocked their
owners, jumping on and off the canvas
walls of the booths, and waving gigantic
fingers across the ceiling.   Past the
tempting stalls streamed the crowd,
past the yellow piles of early oranges,
past barrows of oil-cloth and shell-
fish, artificial flowers, and nuts, books,
sweets, oysters, sparrows, and oleo-
graphs.

In the dark and narrow streets, in
the dimly-lighted alleys that lie round
Brick Lane, the women crouch in
their doorways, each waiting for her
man's return; but on Saturday nights

the younger women throw their shawls aside, and parade up and down the Whitechapel Road, attracted by the life and bustle.

Factory girls, bareheaded and bare-armed, some dressed in gaudy red and blue, marched down the pavement over the snow. Shop-girls, with wonderful curling feathers, and large hollow silver lockets, sauntered along in twos, the baggages! in search of lovers. Girls with happy faces, baggages who had captured lovers, hung on manly arms, and peeped with conscious pride at their companions, with expressions that said that the long-expected hour of the week had come. A dozen young men passed by with the swinging White-chapel gait. As they moved rapidly on, now making a dart at some knot of laughing damsels, now recognizing and calling to some mate in the crowd, as pale-faced and hollow-eyed as themselves, they sang, in derision of the Salvation Army, the chorus :

"To be there ! To be there !
   Oh we know what it is to be there !
   We will come along with you to your sweet
      Salvation home,
   For we know what it is to be there."

Where the road widens into the shape of a racecourse and sends a slanting arm to Hackney, "The Vine Tavern" rises square and bluff, an island off a reef of houses. Patrick and Nina were standing in the shadow of the doorway, and looking down the narrow stone passage, lit by a single naked gas-light. From a room, opening at the further end, came the voices of men in dispute, and the clatter of glass and pewter. Standing in the snow, just without the threshold, the lovers could watch the shadows of the people in the room inside flitting over the red curtain that screened the window close at hand.

A few paces from the inn a blood-red shaft rose tall and heavy in the light of its hanging oil-lamps. Round this beam, sinister as a guillotine, clustered a crowd of men, engaged in a "try your strength" contest, eager to distinguish themselves before the little knot of sweethearts. Man after man took up the heavy wooden hammer and smote with all his might on the peg that sent the wire rattling up to the mark. "One hundred and ninety!" called the proprietor, "that's the way to do it, boys! Have another try. Penny for three trys! Penny for three trys!"

"Why don't ye go and thry, Pat?" said a voice, and Patrick, starting at the sound of his name, saw a pretty, fair-skinned girl urging a red-haired Irishman to go in and win. "Shure, ye can bate all the other bhoys!" Pat, thus implored, took off his coat and

aimed a left-handed blow at the peg.
"Two hundred and sixty!" cried the
marker. Again the Irishman tried, but
this time only scored two hundred and
forty. "Show them what you can do,
sir," suggested the proprietor. Then Pat
braced himself so that the muscles of
his powerful limbs and chest swelled
under his dress, and swinging the heavy
hammer round his head as though it
were a toy, he threw all his weight into
a mighty blow. Nina saw his green
eyes light up, and his red hair flash
in the light, and then the wire sped
up the beam. "Two hundred and
ninety," called the proprietor. "Ten
more, and you could ha' got no farder."
Pat drew on his coat again, and the
fair-skinned girl bore him off, bubbling over with simple pride and delight.

Nina and Patrick turned away from
the inn and walked westward, passing

the old women who sell pigs' trotters
from tiny little tables, dimly illuminated
by candles set in glass chimneys, and
resisting all the temptations that the
owners of shooting-stands and cocoa-
nut pitches, painted sparrows and cower-
ing rabbits offer to the moneyed man.
They scorned the tragedy of "Little Jim,
the Collier's dying Child," and they fled
from the attractions of the Marvel of
the Age, the Boy born with the Head
of a Bull-dog and the Feet of a Frog.
They succumbed, however, to the fas-
cinating rhetoric of a quack medicine
vendor.   Round this worthy's white and
steady flame stood a crowd of solemn-
faced men, drinking in and gravely be-
lieving all the assurances he offered
them.   "I do not offer you these pills,
working men of London," said he,
"without a full knowledge that they
will restore all Wrecks of Humanity to
their usual health!   Working men of

London, if you are ashamed to step forward before all these gentlemen and take these pills and this box of ointment for sixpence, come round to my house this evening, and you shall have them for double the money."

Suddenly Nina drew Patrick's attention away from the working men of London.

"Look at that little tot," said she, and Patrick noticed a tiny little girl trotting along by herself, hugging a loaf of bread in her arms. She was keeping close to the shops so as to avoid being swept away by the streaming crowd. The little creature was absorbed in getting home and in not letting the loaf slip out of her arms. Behind her, in the snow which lay soft and white for a narrow breadth against the houses, could be traced the prints of her feet, four of her wee steps falling within the stride of some man who had gone before her.

"What woman could have the heart to send such a little thing so far in the snow to fetch a loaf!" said Nina. "She cannot be more than five."

She took up the little girl in her arms, and kissed her. The flour from the bottom of the crusty loaf whitened Nina's bosom and filled her fur with dust. The child looked in her face without speaking, and kept a tight hold of the loaf. Her large dark eyes were filled with wonder: "What did the pretty lady want?"

"Look! you baby bunting," said Nina, showing her the ring on her finger.

Then the child gave a faint, shy smile, and putting a little finger between her own faded dress and soft, slender neck, searched for something anxiously. At last she pulled out a string of small blue and white glass beads. It was her little secret, the little secret she kept from the world, and now she smiled triumphantly in the pretty lady's face.

"Oh, you little puss," said Nina. "Let me count!"

But the child looked towards the flaring paraffin of the shooting-stand opposite. The light fell on her tired face, and the bow of her pouting lips, and on her rough brown hair tied with a scrap of orange ribbon. Her wistful look said that somebody was expecting her at home, and that it was time for bed, where, before she fell asleep, with one hand clasping her beloved blue beads, she would think in the darkness of the pretty lady with the fur like a bunny's, and the shining ring.

Nina kissed her wondering eyes, and put her down on the ground, and the child trotted off away into the darkness, hugging the loaf, and keeping close to the wall. Once she looked back towards them, and then making her way through the snow she was lost to sight in the hurrying crowd.

"What a sweet mother you would make, Nina," said Patrick, after a little pause.

She blushed in the darkness, but her heart was glad within her.

"I shall always remember to-night," she said, for the sake of saying something; "it seems very strange, but the roar of the voices here somehow or other brings back the sound of the sea."

"Do you remember that last day we spent at Gixie's Cove," said Patrick, "when we were tired of lying in the deep, cool grass among those silent pines, and we came out of the wood on the hillside furthest from home?"

"How dazzling the sunshine was that afternoon," said Nina. "When we saw the rock standing like marble against that deep blue sky you said in a breath, 'How Greek!' and I, 'How Italian!'"

"And we disputed over which was right; and I said you had never been to Italy; and you said that my Greek was from translations."

"What babies we were!" said Nina. "Still, how we enjoyed the sun, and the air, and the heather."

"And the gorse," added Patrick; "for a mile we plunged knee-deep through the sheet of crimson and yellow slanting away towards the sea. The bees flew out at every step; their low dreamy hum wearied you at last. I believe that was why you wanted to go back."

"It was a little bit their stings," she explained, "but I was thinking of my torn dress half the time. That beautiful furze ruined it, and I would have turned back long before, only I could not bear you to laugh at me again."

Somehow or other Nina was not so much bored with the picturesque as she had been at "The Windsor Castle."

"I wonder if we shall ever see Porlock again," said Patrick. "Let us forget the Mile-End Road for a little, and fancy ourselves back in the deep coombes."

Nina did not speak.

"Shall we?" he asked, eagerly.

"Yes," murmured she, closing her eyes for a moment, and shutting out the black night, and the shadows dancing over the snow, and the endless faces, each so alike, yet each so different.

"At last we left the heather behind," he began, "and ran down the hillside waist-deep in bracken till we came to the short, bare turf with the rock breaking through. The wiry grass was so slippery there that we had to put our feet sideways, and catch at the little hawthorns; and then at the steepest place of all we took off our shoes, and found it quite easy."

"But how clumsy the sheep thought us," she broke in. "They bounded along the narrow runs they had made in the turf, and jumped from ledge to ledge, stopping again, and turning back their stupid white faces to watch us. When you threw stones at them they vanished among the fern, but they always reappeared on some rock higher up the hill."

"At last we came to the bottom of the coombe," he said, doing his best to bring back to her mind the hot August day, and all that had happened, "where the little stream ran down to the sea. At the foot of the slope was a bed of dark green grass which the hill shadow had saved from the sun. There we lay on our faces and drank the water that swirled down in a long, narrow channel over the rushes. There was not a cloud in the sky, though the steep sides of the gorge before and behind shut out so much of it, that we could not be certain; and there was not a single white horse on the sea, which stretched far below us on our right, flashing in the sun till it reached the misty horizon."

He knew that this time she would not say that she always felt a little sentimental on Saturday night, for something in her face told him that he might describe nearly every foot of the cliff they had trodden to Gixie's Cove that day, and yet not weary her.

"The sea looked so near, but we could never get down to it," said Nina. "I think that you might have managed it somehow or other, for I longed to touch the waves."

"I did my very best," said Patrick, piqued; for, in truth, he had climbed down the cliff at that very spot one day when he had not been encumbered with a woman. "I said the only way to manage it was to follow the stream, but we were both

wrong. It was all right till we came to
the oaks where the sunshine came slanting through the boughs, and flecked the
moss on the boulders. It grew darker
and darker lower down, and when we
swung ourselves over that fallen tree
covered with tiny leaved ivy you were
almost afraid to go on. You wouldn't
walk in the water, though it was only a
few inches deep over the slab of rock,
so we climbed the bank again, and came
out clear of the oaks. The sea seemed
just beneath us, and the hill sloped quite
gently for some way till suddenly it
broke off short into the steep cliff. We
tried the stream again, but the brambles
stopped us : those long, yellow flowers,
too, hid the water from us, and when I
trod on them I got wet up to the knee."

"We could not reach the sea, do what
we would," said Nina. "It seemed so
strange to hear it murmuring beneath
us, and then to be forced to go all that

way back again. If we could only have got on to the green slope below, the rest would have been easy.

"That slope was hundreds of feet beneath," he answered. "Don't you remember I threw a stone as high and far as I could, and you watched it, thinking it would drop into the sea? You said it fell half-way down the first slope."

"Well, never mind," said Nina. "What did we do next? I forget."

"You forget!" echoed Patrick, "I shall never forget it. You must remember how instead of going back up the coombe we tried to climb the opposite side, and when we reached those white masses of stones half-way up the hill, we found that though they looked so small from beneath, we could hardly spring from one to the other. I would go on though they got looser and looser, and threatened to slip and crush us, and when we dived under the spreading branches of that oak, we stepped ankle-deep in dead leaves and sticks. How dark it was! You were quite glad to get into the light again."

"Never mind that part," said Nina, quickly. "I know that we went back again; but tell me how we found the way at last."

"Don't you remember how we jumped back across the stream, and though I held out a hand you got one foot soaked with the water?" he asked, lingering on every little detail, because they brought back a thousand sweet memories to him, the sound of her voice, the turn of her head, the mischief in her blue eyes. "And we followed along the bank, past the rushes, and the purple loosestrife till we came to the stone wall.

"And there we saw a black dog come down to drink at the little plank bridge," added Nina. "How it startled me!

I thought we were alone, and so we had been for nearly two hours."

"Curse the dog," muttered Patrick, half to himself. "It was when I——"

"We were quite alone, really," she continued, pretending not to hear him. "The dog was out hunting on its own account, and the farm from which it came was a mile up the valley."

"Well" said Patrick, vying with her as to who could remember the scene the most minutely, "the wall zig-zagged up the hill, and I had to go first to hold back the brambles, for there was only a narrow grassy footpath between the blackberries on the one hand, and the furze on the other. Your dress got so torn that you helped me to knock a stone out of the wall so that you might climb it easily, and get into the cornfield on the other side."

"And it was that which tore it worse than anything else!" said Nina, with a faint laugh. "It was easy to reach the top after once leaving the furze ; and we lay on the sunken earthwork, and we watched the sun sinking into the sea."

"That is not all," said Patrick.

"Oh, there was the mist," said Nina, hurriedly. "There was the mist, of course. It rolled up from the valley beneath, directly the sun set, and we could only see a few yards before us. When we had gone a little way, we could not tell where the sea lay, though we smelt its salt. And then there was the walk home that night along the Mine-head road."

"I wasn't thinking of that," said Patrick, "I was thinking of the two lines from the old Epictetus I read to you in the failing light :—

"' *Some things must be to our dear selves denied
For a short space, some wholly laid aside.*'"

"But that is all past, and we are good

friends now," she said, with a little tremor
in her voice. Then, as Patrick did not
speak, and the silence became too
embarassing. "That is long ago; it
seems so far away now." Her mind was
full of his unaccountable treatment of
her the other night, and she kept repeat-
ing to herself that he had only called
back the past to wound her after all.
Almost unconscious of what she said,
she added—

"I think it is a little cruel——"

"Nina!" cried Patrick, as he saw in
a flash what had been eluding him under
a thousand disguises all the evening,
"Nina!"

Then desperately striving to stave off
the passionate words she was dying to
hear, she added, "But I have forgotten
to tell you the news — Miss Ward is
engaged to Mr. McWhirter. Don't you
hope they'll be happy?"

"What have they to do with us?"

cried Patrick. " Nina——" and at his words everything and everybody else were forgotten. One thought eclipsed the rest ; one word re-echoed in her heart—the world and all that had interested her faded into a background for his love.

By this time the end of the White-chapel Road was reached, and looking back for an instant through the gloom towards the deep orange lights, they heard the hoarse voices of the hawkers, and saw the indistinct masses of figures, passing to and fro before the booths. Then the lovers set their faces westward, and, lost in one another, passed into the darkness towards the silent and deserted streets of the City.

Soon the tired people turned home-wards, and the lights died out one by one, leaving the thickly falling snow to cover up the track beaten hard by so many feet, the tiny steps of the little child who had struggled on with the loaf, and the footprints of the unknown man who had gone before.

THE END.

.

www.ingramcontent.com/pod-product-compliance
Lightning Source LLC
Chambersburg PA
CBHW030824270326
41928CB00007B/883